The Artisan Soul

Also by Erwin Raphael McManus

SOUL CRAVINGS:
An Exploration of the Human Spirit

CHASING DAYLIGHT:
Seize the Power of Every Moment

WIDE AWAKE:
The Future Is Waiting Within You

UPRISING:
A Revolution of the Soul

THE BARBARIAN WAY:
Unleash the Untamed Faith Within

UNLEASHED:
Release the Untamed Faith Within

AN UNSTOPPABLE FORCE:
Daring to Become the Church God Had in Mind

STAND AGAINST THE WIND:
Fuel for the Revolution of Your Soul

The Artisan Soul

Crafting Your Life into a Work of Art

Erwin Raphael McManus

HarperOne
An Imprint of HarperCollinsPublishers

HarperOne

HarperCollins books may be purchased for educational, business, or sales promotional use. For information, please e-mail the Special Markets Department at SPsales@harpercollins.com.

HarperCollins website: http://www.harpercollins.com

HarperCollins®, ♣®, and HarperOne™ are trademarks of HarperCollins Publishers.

FIRST EDITION

Library of Congress Cataloging-in-Publication Data

McManus, Erwin Raphael.
    The artisan soul : crafting your life into a work of art /
Erwin Raphael McManus.—FIRST EDITION.
        p.   cm
    ISBN 978-0-06-227027-6
    1. Christianity and art. 2. Christianity and the arts.
3. Creation (Literary, artistic, etc.)—Religious aspects—
Christianity. 4. Creative ability—Religious aspects—
Christianity. I. Title.
BR115.A8M43   2014
261.5'7—dc23   2013034397

14 15 16 17 18   RRD(H)   10 9 8 7 6 5 4 3 2 1

To Kim, Aaron, and Mariah McManus

Kim, my wife, for thirty years you have journeyed at my side always ready to risk everything to create a better world. Time has only made you more of all the things I treasured when you stole my heart. You are my love.

Aaron, my son, we have known great adventures and fought great battles together you and I. Now as a man you have chosen to return from your journeys and join me for our greatest quest. This is a gift beyond words. You are the fire that burns in the night.

Mariah, my daughter, you are proof that beauty, courage, and wisdom are more than ideals. You have stood by my side and carried both sword and shield—and yet you have always made love your greatest weapon. You lead with an elegance that is rare. You are my warrior poet.

CONTENTS

Soul

The Essence of Art

love Paris. I didn't want to because it seems so
cliché. I have heard Paris described as the most
romantic city in the world. That's hard to argue
with. Strangely though, Paris is romantic even when
you are alone. I have a theory about this—Paris is
a city that romances the human spirit, provokes in
us our imagination, creativity, and love for beauty.
Everywhere you look you are surrounded by beauty.
The sounds and smells are both soothing and exhilarating. Even the language is beautiful. The Eiffel

Tower seems like an ancient marker to let everyone know that if you're an artist then this is home. If there is a city that personifies the artisan soul, one could make a strong argument that Paris is it. Paris is what a city looks like when artists create it. I feel more artistic when I am in Paris.

After one particular weeklong visit with my wife, Kim, she asked me on the last day while we were enjoying our final breakfast in the middle of the world's most romantic city, "We're moving here, aren't we?" I was surprised by how direct her question was. She could feel what was happening inside of me, and I must admit when we flew back home I left a part of myself in the City of Light. I had an affair with Paris, but I love Los Angeles.

I live in the City of Angels. I live in the heart of Los Angeles, California. Every day I am reminded of how much Paris and Los Angeles have in common. I live in a world of artists. Los Angeles has the highest concentration of professional artists of any city in the world. As I walk the six blocks from my house to Larchmont Village for a cup of coffee, I pass an endless number of writers, designers, actors, directors, dancers, painters—you name it. If you sit down to drink a cappuccino, all around you will hear conversations about their next great creative endeavors, the stories they are working on, the films they are making, the plays they are writing, or the sets they are designing. It all reminds me of the immense capacity of the human imagination when leveraged with talent, skill, and hard work. It's no wonder that Los Angeles has been described as the capital of creativity. Once the *Los Angeles Times* described Los Angeles's number one export as creativity itself.

We live in the shadow of the iconic sign that once read "Hollywoodland." Yet, strangely enough, most of these artists were not born here. They come from everywhere, from Detroit and Des Moines, from Atlanta and Albany.

No matter where we are, we live in a world of artists. While it is clear that world-class cities draw world-class talent, it is equally clear that world-class talent comes from everywhere. Megacities rank high in human attributes like intellect, education, and creativity. This could lead us to a false impression of the limited commodity of human creativity. The reality is that big cities pillage small towns by making themselves more attractive to those who are most keenly aware of their talent and take on the discipline to refine it.

While I live in a world of artists and am also keenly aware that artists live all over the world, the artisan soul goes much deeper than simply those who understand themselves as artists and are pursuing careers in an overtly creative field. I have come to realize, after over thirty years of studying human creativity, that the great divide is not between those who are artists and those who are not, but between those who understand that they are creative and those who have become convinced that they are not. The great divide is between those who understand that their very nature is that of an artist and those who remain unaware or in denial of their artisan soul.

The tragedy, of course, is that most of us have never thought of ourselves as artists. Most of us live our lives convinced that we are uncreative. Most of us have spent our lives admiring those who have the gift of creativity while seeing our role as simply celebrating their uniqueness.

Words reveal our values and culture. The more familiar we are with something, the more words we have to describe it. The more common something is, the more nuanced our language and detail becomes. When we describe someone as creative, imaginative, or artistic, we often lack clarity because we consider ourselves none of the above. When we think of artists we tend to think of them as a rare and elite category of people. While great art inspires us all, it also has a subtle way of diminishing us. We create an unconscious category that separates them from the rest of us. Their creativity is proof that we are not creative; their artistry proof that we are not artistic. Yet what humanity needs most is for us to set creativity free from this singular category of the extraordinary and release it into the hands of the ordinary. Creativity should be an everyday experience. Creativity should be as common as breathing. We breathe, therefore we create.

I rarely find anyone who would answer the question "Are you creative?" with a resounding yes. Even those who say yes do so sheepishly. Somewhere along the way, we were told that creativity is a gift given to a rare and elite few. The rest of us have to struggle through life doing the best we can with the little bit we've been given. What makes things worse is that this framework is reinforced by the commonly held beliefs of sincere people of faith.

After breaking the shackles that have held our creative essence captive for far too long, let us never relinquish our rights as creatives and creators. A soul that is free and alive is a soul that creates. We need not only a new view of God but a new view of us. We need a new theology and a new anthropology. Humans create.

Over twenty years ago, I found myself in the middle of this conversation in the context of both anthropology and theology. An anthropological question was at its core: What is it that makes us human? Is every human being inherently creative? The theological dilemma was even deeper: Is creativity an activity that singularly belongs to God? There seemed to be an underlying assumption that any engagement in the creative act was an act of defiance against God the Creator. In practical terms, this has played out in the church over the last thousand years. Faith and creativity seemed to be adversaries rather than allies. In the church, spirituality and creativity seemed to be at war rather than acting as kindred spirits.

I remember the controversy that began when Mosaic, our community of faith in Los Angeles, established as one of its core values that creativity is the natural result of spirituality. I have to confess that when I penned this phrase I was completely oblivious to the tremendous push back I would receive. The integration of spirituality and creativity was as obvious from my perspective as the relationship between inhaling and exhaling. The push back came in various forms and, if I might say, from incredibly creative angles.

One leader in the Christian movement tried to restrain me by explaining that I was putting undue pressure on people by requiring that their spirituality somehow manifest itself in creativity. From her perspective, establishing creativity as a basic expression of being human would doom most people to failure.

And let me be clear on this point—she was exactly right! But it was for exactly the wrong reasons.

Her view is that most of us are simply not creative.

Aspiring to be something we are not leads only to failure. This is exactly wrong. But she was right about the reality of failure when we embrace this new view of ourselves. It takes courage to not only accept our limitations but embrace our potential. To deny our creative nature is to choose a life where we are less and thus responsible for less. We see ourselves as created beings, so we choose to survive. When we see ourselves as creative beings, we must instead create.

If we are inherently spiritual creatures, we are by our nature creative beings, yet we live in the fear that if we aspire to be more we will discover ourselves to be less. We live in fear of failure, convinced that failure will prove us to be frauds. We have bought into the lie that creative people never fail and hence failure is proof that we are not creative. So we get back in line, our dreams in check, and condemn our souls to a slow and painful death.

Fear is the shadow of creativity. When we choose to create, we bring light to our fears. The darkness does not prevail over us. The creative act is inherently an act of courage. We are born to far too many fears and far too great a darkness. It is only when we find the courage to create that we are freed from those fears and that darkness. The past will be our future until we have the courage to create a new one. To make our lives a creative act is to marry ourselves to risk and failure.

True creativity does not come easily; creativity is born of risk and refined from failure. If we are at the core both spiritual beings and creative beings, then the artisan soul is where we live when we have the courage to be our truest selves.

This is the courage of the artisan—to know ourselves and be true to that knowledge. The artisan rejects all that makes us false and takes the huge risk of being true. To embrace our authentic selves and live in that raw expression of being fully human is our greatest risk and our richest reward.

We fear because we are uncertain that we are enough.

We fear because we are certain that we are not enough.

We fear because the creative act calls us to be more than we can be alone.

We fear because we were never intended to create apart from God.

We are like children with nuclear fusion in our hands—never fully grasping our potential for good and for destruction. It's easier to control people if we convince them that they are inherently uncreative—everyone simply conforms and cooperates. If we want to create a better world, we had better start to unleash the creative potential inside each person to create all that is good and beautiful and true.

I love the reminder that "perfect love drives out fear" (1 John 4:18).

There is an order to the creative process: we dream, we risk, we create.

We cannot create without risk.

There is no riskier way of life than the artisan way. Anything less is just existing.

Another significant faith leader was more poignant in his response. I still remember his words (frankly, they are pretty hard to forget): "People are worker bees. They simply need a task to be happy. Our singular task as followers of Christ is to obey, not to create."

I know this seems straightforward. After all, how do we argue with that last statement? Unless, of course, we are commanded to create. Unless, of course, we are created to create. What if the creative act is not an act against nature but an expression of our nature? What if the creative act is not an act against God but a reflection of his image within us? Honestly, I still get a knot in my stomach when I think of human beings being described as worker bees, but what bothers me more is when I see this philosophy played out all over the world in countless numbers of lives.

Too many believe the lie that God commands and humans obey. It's just not that simple. This view is destructive and demeaning, a distortion of God's intention for humanity.

To create is to be human.

To create is to fulfill our divine intention.

To create is to reflect the image of God.

To create is an act of worship.

So, who is an artist? Anyone who has a soul. What are the qualifications for being an artist? You guessed it—having a soul. And though we celebrate the way the artisan soul is expressed in those who bring artistry and beauty to the world, this book is not about how to turn yourself into a painter or a dancer or an actor or a writer. Instead, this book is about a process through which you will discover and unleash your personal creativity. For us to journey together, we have to come together with the basic assumption that each human being is uniquely designed to be part of the creative act. To move forward together, we have to realize that life itself is a work of art.

When I first mentioned to my wife, Kim, that I was beginning work on *The Artisan Soul,* her immediate and unfiltered response was, "I'm glad you're doing something that works for you since you're an artist, but it doesn't really work for people like me." Let me be clear, *The Artisan Soul* is for everyone who cannot escape the gnawing realization that their life is unfulfilled. It is for everyone who knows their life is meant for more than survival or even success. *The Artisan Soul* is for everyone who knows that "doing" is not enough to satisfy our deepest longings and who is desperate to live a life about being. The irony, of course, is that Kim is one of the most creative and artistic people you will ever meet. But somewhere in her past Kim believed a lie she was told—that she was not an artist, that she was not creative, that she was just normal, ordinary, common. I can say as confidently about you as I can about Kim that there is nothing common or ordinary about you.

My son, Aaron, came to me years ago, when he was transitioning from a boy to a man, and said he was unsure if he could join Mosaic. I asked him, with deep concern and confusion, why he felt that way. He said he didn't know if he could embrace our fifth core value: *Creativity is a natural result of spirituality.* He said, "Dad, you have to remember, I spent a few years in a Christian school, and all I have to say is there were some very spiritual people there, and it was an incredibly uncreative place."

Maybe you're like Aaron. You have seen lots of evidence that not only are spirituality and creativity not inseparable, but in fact they rarely come together. But this is less than the ideal God intended.

Love is the defining mark of the church, but we have far too often fallen short of that mark. Still, we do not give up on love. We continue to make it our ideal. We understand that this is God's standard. We are most human when love is our motive. It is the same with creativity. God created us through the universe's most creative and intimate act. We are the result of a creative act by a creative God. He designed us in his own image; he designed us with both intellect and imagination; he designed us with both reason and passion; he designed us to dream, to risk, and to create.

The church's lack of creativity should never be used to argue that creativity is not our most spiritual act. We must instead go back to the beginning and remind ourselves of who we really are. Art exists to remind us that we have a soul, and all we need to be an artist is a soul.

There are various ways to define the soul, but they always involve an attempt to describe the essence of being human, which separates us from other species. The soul is the aspect of being human that drives our imagination, emotions, and thoughts toward the highest ideals of what it means to be human.

The soul is the part of us that longs for and connects to the transcendent.

Our soul is the space that contains the universe within us.

The soul is the creative space from which humans create the future.

The soul is the essence of being human.

Though we may create many beautiful works of art, the most important works of art to which we will ever give ourselves are the lives we live. No matter what else we produce in life—whether we are painters or filmmakers or dancers or poets, even if we create something that might someday be kept in a gallery or museum somewhere in the world for generations of people to come and marvel at the wonder of our work—we will never create anything more powerful or significant than our lives. The complexity is that we are both works of art and artists at work. At first, our soul is like a canvas where others begin to paint the portrait of who we are. Slowly, as we develop and mature, we take the brush into our own hands and continue painting our own lives. Then we go beyond that, to leave our mark on the world around us. We don't have to convince children that they are creative; all we have to do is let them do what comes naturally. We never have to give a four-year-old permission to color outside the lines or to not follow the rules or to simply draw on the page what they see in their imagination. Yet somewhere along the way, this gets restructured. We become convinced that only those who are drawing inside the lines are doing it right, that the rules are more important than anything else, that we can't possibly allow our unfiltered imagination to be reflected in reality. Creativity is replaced with conformity; originality is replaced with standardization.

We might wonder if it even matters what we think of ourselves. Is it really that critical to embrace the artist within us? I would simply remind you of the insight from the Scriptures: as a man thinks, so is he.

Have you ever been around a person who has

chosen to truly engage with a job, investing all his or her creative potential, against the backdrop of all those who are simply doing a good job to make it through the day? Did you ever have a teacher in school who took the life out of literature or made history into mundane memorization of meaningless facts and dates? I know I did. In fact, children everywhere have been the victims of teachers who have sucked the imagination out of whatever subject was sadly entrusted to them.

I have also experienced the wonder of sitting in classrooms with teachers who saw education as an opportunity to express their full creative potential. Filling us with imagination and inspiration, they provoked us to learn and grow. I sat in a master's-level Greek class with Dr. Thomas Urrey, whose eyes filled with tears as he read in Greek from Ephesians. I had rarely felt so inspired in the classroom. I went home and told my wife, Kim, that I could not give that man anything less than my very best and that he deserved an A from me.

Kim is an extraordinary educator. I would walk into her classroom to find third graders sitting in a part of the room that looked like an imperial throne, others reading in an ark they had built, and still others studying in a fanciful jungle. Every semester Kim's classroom was an explosion of imagination, creativity, beauty, and wonder. Every student who walked into her room discovered the love of learning.

Have you ever had the misfortune of going to a dentist who was uninspired by his profession? I have never been able to get images from the movie *Marathon Man* out of my brain. If you are too young to remember, it stars Dustin Hoffman and features the single worst encounter with a dentist known to mankind. Watch that movie and you will let your teeth rot out before you allow a dentist to say, "Open wide." I am absolutely certain I have been to dentists that are direct descendants of the one in *Marathon Man*. I have lived my life in fear of dentists and have probably paid the consequences.

Fortunately, in the last few years I have been given the gift of not one but two dentists who saw dentistry as the context of their creativity. The first was Dr. Dan Romo, who is listed on the Strengths-Finder assessment as having the primary strength of empathy. In his practice, they give you a headset playing music that you enjoy, dip your hands in hot wax to reduce your stress (leaving you with very soft hands), speak in calm, soothing voices, and somehow make dental work nothing less than a work of art. Dan Romo is a poet with a drill, and I am grateful that I could be his canvas.

My present dentist, who sings to the music playing over the intercom while performing oral surgery, is as careful to minimize your pain as he is to maximize the aesthetic quality of his work. On my last visit, he informed me that he also designs bow ties. Suddenly it all made sense. My dentist is an artist; for him, dentistry is simply the context for him to express his artisan soul.

Far too many of us have had the misfortune of working for companies whose values reflect a utilitarian philosophy and a view of people as commodities. Far too many of us live in a dehumanizing context where standardization and conformity are the measures of a good employee. And just as many of us have experienced that at our places of work, even more have experienced it in their places of worship. How did it happen that religion and conformity became bedfellows? Far too often, spirituality has been replaced with standardization, and discovering the unique divine image within each person is replaced with a version of discipleship from the Industrial Revolution. I have met many people whose search for God ended in disappointment when they found themselves losing their humanity rather than discovering what it means to be fully human.

What gives me great hope is the number of companies that have broken away from the Industrial Revolution vision of people as cogs in a wheel to see people as the organization's greatest resource. All over the world, companies and organizations are radically redefining work as a place where people no longer simply fill a slot but are empowered to bring their best selves and unlock their full creative potential. I am thrilled to discover that communities of faith have also made this transition. All around, it seems, there are churches that understand discipleship to be not a system of conformity but a process of unleashing the creative potential in each person.

Ironically, this concept should not be foreign to the church, since Paul wrote two thousand years ago that each person is given different gifts and each of us has a unique place in service and a unique part to play. The Scriptures have never been about conformity, and certainly Jesus's early movement was never described in terms of standardization. Jesus's early followers formed a movement of dreamers and visionaries. It's exciting to consider where this kind of framework could lead. What would happen if the closer we got to God, the more we discovered our full creative potential? What would happen if the deeper and more profound our spiritual journey, the more we felt free to express our creative essence and embrace our personal uniqueness?

When we are freed from the rules and regulations that are so often imposed on us in the name of God, we discover that creativity is the natural result of spirituality. And if this is true, then our soul is the primary material for all artistic expression. In other words, we create out of being.

All art is an expression and extension of ourselves. There may be no virtue more admired by those who understand themselves as artists than authenticity. Art finds its deepest value when it is the authentic expression of a deep human experience. Art becomes profound when it exposes us, explains us, or inspires us. We have all experienced artistic expressions that somehow left us flat and unmoved. We instinctively know when a film or a painting or a song is essentially soulless. Yet there is something breathtaking about a work that is genuinely original and authentic to the artist. We may not always have the language to explain it, but somehow we know the difference between art and imitation. And though we may be fooled from time to time, most of us quickly learn to distinguish between art and propaganda.

Art in its purest form is an extension of the soul. This is exactly what life is supposed to be. Which leads us to this realization: the only art we can create is that which authentically reflects who we are. Our soul is the material for all we create. Thus, to nurture the artisan soul, essence is far more important than talent.

Jim Collins has done us a great service and inspired a great many of us through his work *Good to Great*. Certainly we should all aspire to reach our highest level of execution, both personally and organizationally. Note that the journey he recommends is from good to great—not from bad to great or from evil to great. Even in the journey to greatness, the assumed starting point is that we have already found our way to good.

Collins points out the importance of moving to a level of excellence that elevates an organization beyond the life of its founder. He gives us keen insights into sustainability and leadership. These are critical insights, but context matters in the use of this language.

There is a subtle side effect when it comes to the language of *good* and *great*. *Good* has become less than *great*. *Good* has become "above average." *Good to great* has become the same as *better to best,* when in fact they are of different qualities altogether when it comes to essence.

The linguistic dilemma is that we have an inclination to relegate the word *good* to a secondary state of being that is inferior to greatness. The contrast reinforces a critical misperception about the nature of *good*. We need to rediscover the essential nature of the good.

Great is about execution and achievement; *good* is about essence and ethos. The artisan soul aspires to do great work but never neglects the importance of being inspired by all that is good and beautiful.

When it comes to the soul and the creation of life as a work of art, the danger is to aspire to greatness while neglecting the critical nature of the good.

It has always fascinated me that in the first and preeminent act of creation, the focus was on the good and not the great. In Genesis 1, we find ourselves in the moment when God creates everything out of nothing. The all-too-familiar six days could be better described as six movements, six motions within a single creative act. God begins by creating light out of darkness and finishes by breathing life into man. Everything in between is nothing less than extraordinary. Within each movement, there is a single intention, whether it is the creation of the solar system or the unique design of this planet's ecosystem. Every stroke within this creative act carries the intention of creating life. Every creative act for which we can take responsibility pales in comparison to the wonder and power of the revelation of God's immense creativity as demonstrated in creation. As impressive as creation is, however, it is not once described as "great." Yet certainly, if anything deserved the designation of greatness, it would be this work of art. Instead, at the end of each day, at the point of reflection and evaluation, for each stroke there is one simple summarizing description for the nature of all that just happened: "And God saw that it was good."

Seven times in this first chapter of Genesis, interwoven into the narrative of creation, we are brought back to the simple phrase "It was good." It seems as if the intent of the writer of Genesis is that we not miss the significance of this point. Everything God created was good. The word *good* is used five times in Genesis 2 and three times in Genesis 3, suggesting a subtle narrative that as humanity moved away from God, it moved away from the source of all things good.

Describing each phase of creation as good seems like a gross understatement. I have to admit that I have done one or two things in my life that I thought were better than good, a couple of things I thought might even have touched great, but I have to re-think that against the backdrop of creation being de-scribed as good and not great. At the very least, this is incredible restraint when it comes to giving out compliments. Can you imagine describing the *Mona Lisa* as good rather than magnificent? Or describing van Gogh's *The Starry Night* as good rather than exquisite?

It could be that this tells us a lot about the dif-ference between who God is and who we are. For most of us, being great is far more important than being good. Being great is most often a description of our talent, but being good is poignantly connected to our essence. Obviously creation was great, but it is far more important for us to understand that cre-ation is the reflection of the very nature of God. Remember, we can create only out of who we are, and everything we create is a reflection of who we are. So it makes perfect sense that all of creation, every stroke of the creative act, ended with an emphatic declaration that it was good. Creation was good because God is good. Creation resulted in life because God is life.

From the very beginning, the Scriptures describe God as an artist. At his core God is an artisan. On the seventh day he rested not from his work of engineering or his work of teaching or his work of administrating, but from his work of creating. Granted, there was in creation extraordinary engineering, profound teaching, and no small amount of administration. The point is not to contrast these actions, but that all those things happened within the creative act.

It is important to note that even in creation the culminating moment of the creative act emerged when creativity reached its point of deepest intimacy. Six times it was good enough to describe creation as good. But the seventh reference, the seventh occasion where God describes creation as good, is directly connected to his decision to create humanity in his image. It was only when God created us that he upgraded the compliment and said not only that it was good, but that it was very good. To bring light out of darkness, God needed only to speak, but to bring his image alive in humanity, he needed to breathe his life directly into our lungs. The description could not be more intimate or personal: "The Lord God formed a man from the dust of the ground and breathed into his nostrils the breath of life, and the man became a living being" (Genesis 2:7).

Our story begins with a kiss, mouth-to-mouth resuscitation, God pressing against us. We begin when God exhales and we inhale. This is the level of intimacy and synchronicity for which we were always intended. While all creation declares the glory of God, we humans bear the image of God. The more clearly we reflect the divine, the more we reflect that which is good and beautiful and true. Again, all creation is good because God is good. The entire universe reflects God's essence. God creates out of who he is, and when we are aligned with him, everything we create brings him honor and glory. Imagine what the world would look like if all of us in our essence reflected this most extraordinary good, and everything we created was an extension of that beauty. I love the fact that the same Hebrew word that is translated as "good" is in other places simply translated as "beautiful."

You are an artist. You were created with an artisan soul. The question is: What kind of art will you leave behind? The reason it is critical to go all the way back to the beginning is that sometimes we get trapped in the past rather than at the beginning. Most of us are still in some small way victims of the Industrial Revolution, whether through our grandparents', our parents', or our own experience. We were raised to believe that our place in life required compliance and conformity rather than creativity and uniqueness. We have been raised in a world where information is deemed far more important than imagination. Adults replaced dreams with discipline when they were finally ready to grow up and be responsible for their lives.

Whether this construct was reinforced on an assembly line, in a cubicle, or in a classroom, the surest path to acceptance in society is accepting standardization, and we more than willingly relinquish our uniqueness. I have wondered if it was actually easier before the Industrial Revolution to understand our relationship with the creative process. Farmers, after all, understood the direct relationship between hard work and creation. They worked the soil; they planted the seeds; they watered the crops; and they watched life happen. They understood that they were integral to the creative act, even though few farmers would have described it that way.

The same could be said for any number of craftsmen—the cobbler, the blacksmith, the carpenter. Their livelihood was not far removed from simple expression of their artistry. I have heard it said that Henry Ford once mused that people can have a

Model T in any color they want as long as it's black. This is probably the best summary of the worldview of the Industrial Revolution. Everyone can have it exactly like they want it as long as they want it exactly the way it is. The ideal utopian society is a world where everyone and everything are the same.

Years ago we at Mosaic created a developmental process for leaders, called Yelo. We involved such assessments as the Myers-Briggs Type Indicator, StrengthsFinder, and the Character Matrix from my book *Uprising*. The name, though obscure, had real meaning. I would walk into a room of absolute strangers, write a color on my hand, and then tell them we were going to create a cultural color from among the group. Whether there were fifty people in the room or five hundred, it always turned out the same. I would have all the groups seated at tables in groups of eight to ten. Each person was asked to write down his or her favorite color and second-favorite color. Go ahead and do that right now as you are reading.

Then I would have everyone reveal their first choice to the group, and if the majority agreed on a color, that would be the group's color. If there was a tie, they would then move to secondary preferences to determine the group's color. Then I would have the groups of eight to ten merge with other groups, and those groups went through the same process to determine the group's principal color. By the time the process was complete, no matter how individuals began—and there are always individuals who pick anything from orange to silver, from purple to green, from black to white—without exception, everywhere I have traveled, the culture color was blue.

Strangely enough, studies show that blue is the preferred eye color of over 80 percent of people, and over half those surveyed choose blue as their favorite color. When blue is not their favorite color, it is often their second favorite. When people choose what color to wear, blue is once again the dominant choice (just think blue jeans). Pay attention to the main characters in television shows. The characters you are supposed to empathize with frequently wear blue. For whatever reason—maybe it's the imprint of living on the blue planet—blue wins hands down.

Once the room has gone through this rigorous and tumultuous process, and we discover that the cultural color is blue, I have someone come and read the word that I wrote in ink on my hand before the process began. To the dismay of the room, the volunteer reads out loud, "Blue." Everyone is shocked that I knew beforehand the cultural color of the room. Part of the learning process is talking to the people whose favorite color is red or aqua or yellow about how it felt to abandon their preference so they could belong to the whole—how it felt to have to stand up in a room and, instead of proudly saying "I am pink," to join the majority in declaring blue. For some, neither their primary nor secondary choice is blue. For them, strangely enough, the experience becomes profoundly visceral, a moment of realization that they are being stripped of their uniqueness, their core self. But in reality they have lost nothing. It's just an exercise. They can reclaim their silver and black the moment the exercise is over.

Of course, this is the whole point of the exercise. We are creatures who live in tension between blue and yellow. All of us, whether we admit it or not, want to be at least in part blue. We want to be accepted; we want to belong; we want to have things in common with those whose opinions we care about. But we also want to be yellow. We want to preserve our uniqueness; we want to be uncommon. We hope that in some small way we can be original.

It's kind of ironic that if we mix blue and yellow, we get green, because in our most unhealthy state we become green envying those who are naturally blue, who easily fit into the expectations of the majority and win their admiration and affection. At the same time, we are envious of those who have the courage to stand apart in their own yellow space, who seem comfortable as iconoclasts and somehow have risen above their need to be accepted by the majority to leave a unique mark on the world.

When the Industrial Revolution pulled us out of an

era fraught with difficulties and challenges we hope
to never face again, it also stripped us of a core part
of our humanity that we need to reclaim. Let me be
clear: good things happen when we find a blue space
where we can all walk together, where we can share
common goals and values and be united by what
makes us the same rather than standing apart because of what makes us different. Certainly I am not
advocating that we all be different for difference's
sake. There is no virtue in being out of step with
others for the sole purpose of walking alone. The artisan soul is not about rebellion but about resonance.
It is about being true to who we are and allowing that
truth to inform and form us.

After Kim's initial push back on the theme of the
artisan soul, I asked her if anything about being an
artisan appealed to her. She said, "Yeah. Artisan
bread. I like artisan bread," which roused my curiosity. What exactly is artisan bread? What is bread
when it is not artisan bread? What are the distinc-
tions and characteristics of artisan bread, and do
these characteristics translate to the artisan soul?

What I expected to find was quite the opposite of
what I did find. Somehow I thought that I would have
to weave my way like a secret agent through the artisan bread community to find someone willing to
divulge secrets. If artisan bread is better than nonartisan bread, certainly the process and the ingre-

dients would be locked in a vault somewhere. After all, in this cannibalistic and venture-capitalist world there are an endless number of corporate vultures ready to steal the homegrown secrets of the independent artisan.

Without knowing much about bread, I did have a sense that whenever something is described as "artisan," it is usually identified with something small and local and intimate. What I found was quite a pleasant surprise. The secrets of artisan bread were readily available. I expected an endless number of secret ingredients, several of which I could not pronounce, but I found quite the opposite. The ingredients were simple and pure, four to be exact: yeast, flour, salt, and water. As best I can tell, those ingredients are available to everyone. Nonartisan bread, in contrast, normally has more than twenty ingredients, many not easily recognizable and impossible to pronounce. The defining characteristic of artisan bread is that the ingredients are simple and pure— pure in their essence—and everything goes in the direction of simplicity.

The second characteristic of artisan bread is the process. Here you find the distinction between artisan and not. Artisan bread is the result of a craft; nonartisan bread is nothing more than a product. The process distinguishes what is mass-produced from what is crafted and created. For a bread to be considered artisan, it must be handcrafted. Artisan bread comes from a process and environment that reflect imagination and intimacy. Artisan bread is normally crafted in small bakeries with small ovens and is always the result of an artisan's personal touch. With artisan bread, no two loaves of bread ever look the same.

It strikes me that this may explain why so many people I have talked to over the years have such a visceral resistance to what they would describe as megachurches. Far too often the megachurch experience moves from a process that is intimate and hands-on to a process that feels mass-produced. The truth is that many megachurches are far more committed to intimacy and simplicity than small churches that are closed to outsiders. But the point remains: the human spirit, as it moves toward spiritual health, knows intrinsically that the artisan process is better for the soul than any process that moves toward mass production.

The artisan soul moves toward purity of ingredients, understands the power of simplicity, makes life a craft and not a product, and treats people as unique individuals rather than commodities. The artisan process reminds me of God's words to Jeremiah in chapter 18: "'Go down to the potter's house, and there I will give you my message.' So I went down to the potter's house, and I saw him working at the wheel. But the pot he was shaping from the clay was marred in his hands; so the potter formed it into another pot, shaping it as seemed best to him." Later God describes to Jeremiah his relationship to his people: "Like clay in the hand of the potter, so are you in my hand" (18:6).

Sometimes the hand of God presses against us and creates unwanted discomfort. Like clay in the hands of a potter, we may feel God's pressing against us as intrusive and disruptive, but we must never lose sight of the fact that God never chooses to give up on us or to put us on an assembly line and treat us as a commodity. He always presses against us. His process is always hands-on. And with each of us he avoids standardization, working to form each person into a unique image of God.

If this is the process that God chooses with us, if God refuses to mass-produce but insists on an intimate process that in the end forms each of us into the image of Christ, why would we choose a lesser path for our own lives? The work of the artist begins with the care of his or her own soul. Remember, God didn't have to make everything he created good; everything he created was good because he made it.

This is the beauty of the artisan way. Once we've cared for our souls, once we've dealt with the essence of who we are, once our focus is on our being, everything that emanates from us will naturally result in the good and the beautiful and the true. The problem, of course, is that this process takes time and requires touch, like the artisan bread that depends on the artist being willing to wait. Artists understand that the process of fermentation cannot be rushed or hurried. They know that the products they are committed to creating will not happen if they take shortcuts or circumvent the process, and so it is with our soul. For our lives to be works of art, we need to allow a lifetime of work. We must give God the time to make us works of art. We must press close to God and allow both the tenderness of his touch and the pressure of his hands to shape us and mold us into someone we would not be without him. If we want our lives to be works of art, we must be willing to take the time and risk the intimacy required for creating an artisan life. We have to get close enough to allow the hands of God to press against us and reform us.

The creative act began with God creating the universe in which we live. The next creative act begins when we allow God to re-create the universe within us.

In Ezekiel 36:26–27, God says, "I will give you a new heart and put a new spirit in you. I will remove from you your heart of stone and give you a heart of flesh. And I will put my spirit in you and move you to follow my decrees and be careful to keep my laws."

The same God who creates, re-creates. And that process of re-creation begins in our very souls. Paul said it like this in 2 Corinthians 5:17: "Therefore, if anyone is in Christ, the new creation has come: The old has gone, the new is here!"

Years ago I sat with a friend who was an incredibly gifted artist. He was at the beginning of his career and felt an overwhelming angst about what it meant to be a steward of his talent and at the same time make a living. He complained that every job opportunity felt to him like an offer to sell out. He felt that companies offering commissions did not want him to express true emotions through his art. He said they only wanted him as a machine to advance propaganda and advocate emotions that were not authentic or genuine to the human experience. I asked him to give me an example. He quickly said, "They want me to create art that advocates success, happiness, love, rather than true and authentic emotions like anger, betrayal, fear."

As I listened, I was struck by a powerful realization that has never left me. Every true artist fights for their authenticity. Nothing feels more demeaning or degrading than creating art that is a false expression of the self. I realized in that moment that the only emotions which were real to him, the only emotions that felt truly human, were the ones that reflect our most broken selves. His art most naturally was informed by the dark and empty places of the human soul.

I paused and asked him what I thought was an obvious question. I said, "Is it possible that emotions like love or even happiness could be true human experiences and authentic expressions of what it means to be human?"

He was a very thoughtful person and rarely answered impetuously. I could see him reflecting and processing. It was as if he was going through the catalog of all his life experiences. And after a moment, he looked at me and said, "That thought had never occurred to me."

I felt the pain of that moment, the honest realization that neither happiness nor love felt like places human beings could speak from authentically. He was a young man when we had that conversation, just past twenty years old. He never made it to forty. In a moment of despair, he ended his life, leaving behind hundreds of friends and family who loved him and believed in his future.

This brilliant artist couldn't find an authentic place in his soul to remind him that life was worth living.

This journey that I am inviting you on, this path that I hope to provoke you to begin to walk, is not an easy one. The journey will demand much of you.

In fact, it will demand all of you. All your passion. All your courage. All your talent. All your discipline. All your life.

The way of the artisan is a life in which we risk all for love. The artisan embraces the dangers that come from living an authentic life and still chooses to live unguarded from the pain of the wounds of love.

Artists love without reservation. They give their hearts completely and leave nothing on the table. They are naked and unashamed. They leave no room for pretension. And because they have given all of themselves, they live without regret.

But not without struggle. This path is not an escape from life's wounds and disappointment. To live from our souls is to pursue our greatest passions and expose ourselves to our greatest pain. We cannot live to create and be surprised that we have traveled through failure. We cannot live a life of passion and not know sorrow. To pursue a dream is to invite a nightmare! To live a life of love is to know betrayal and loss. The soul is both fragile and resilient. The artisan soul embraces the essential nature of both vulnerability and efficacy. All creativity emerges from struggle. All art is born out of the pain of labor. The artisan soul must be both tender and tough.

So let me be clear—what I am inviting you to is the path of most resistance, with the most risk and the most reward. It is not for the faint of heart or for those who long for safety and security. The way of the artisan is not an invitation to sit in the sun enjoying a cool summer's breeze, imagining a better life and a better world. It is about embracing our creative power and responsibility to create the life and the world that our soul inspires us to imagine.

This process is both creativity and responsibility. It is both imaginative and pragmatic. The intent of this book is to change both the way you see yourself and your relationship to the creative process. The future is a creative act, and like any creative act, the tools are as essential as the process. This is why in the final pages you will find a section entitled "Anvil and Hammer." This section is waiting for you the moment you are ready to ask the question, "So what do I do now?" You can either absorb a chapter and then move right to the end of the book to pick up your anvil and hammer or you can work through the entire book first. Once you have embraced your artisan soul, you will begin the hard work of turning your life into a work of art. Don't underestimate the depth of this section because of its brevity. It is through the anvil and hammer that you will fully engage your creative potential.

If you begin this journey recognizing that all art is an expression of your essence and that your most treasured possession is the health of your soul, then I know without question that something beautiful can come from this quest.

He who is the Creator God is the creative God, and he created us in his image and likeness. He created us with imagination and curiosity, with the capacity to hope and dream, and he placed within us all the material necessary to live an extraordinarily creative life. The proof is that more than anything else we are a soul, and that soul is the divine material with which we are made to create. The difference between humans and every other species on this planet is that humans are artists. This is our uniqueness—we were created to create.

Somewhere along the way we forgot this. We became convinced we were something less. It is time to become more.

I have seen the future, and it is filled with beauty and wonder.

That's what happens when humans embrace their artisan souls and begin to create.

To create is to be fully human.

We stand at the precipice of a revolution of creativity; the beginning of a new renaissance.

We live in a world of artists.

Voice

The Narrative That Guides

When I was a small boy living in El Salvador, a painting hung on the most prominent wall of our home. It was a singular work of art that my grandparents seemed so proud of. When I asked where it came from, they explained that it was a masterpiece painted by my aunt. It was a beautiful painting with deep religious sentiment—a painting of Jesus with his twelve disciples sitting around a table sharing the Last Supper. I remember looking at that painting time and again, wondering how my aunt imagined such a beautiful scene. You can imagine my dismay when years later I discovered it was actually Leonardo da Vinci's painting *The Last Supper*.

It seems my aunt was given a paint-by-numbers art kit when she was younger. In its preeminent place in our home, it reflected more her parents' admiration of her than any sense of the quality or uniqueness of the original. All she had to do was apply the right color to the right numbered section, carefully staying inside the lines, and then leave it out to dry. Ironically the frame was probably worth more than the painting. I'm not saying my aunt didn't have talent—in fact, it may be that this was only a first step in the expression of her own artistic soul—but even the uninformed novice would understand that there is a universe of difference between Aunt Alma's *Last Supper* and the one that came from the imagination of Leonardo da Vinci.

There is a stark difference between art and imitation. Not that imitation is a bad thing. Even an authentic creative journey begins with imitation. It's how we learn everything. It's how we learn language: we hear sounds and begin to make the connection between sound and meaning. At first all language is just imitation. It is echoing others' voices and embracing without reflection the meaning the sounds hold.

My first language was Spanish, passed on to me

mostly from my grandparents during my years in El Salvador. My primary language is now English. That came later, while going to school in Miami, Florida. The first language came more naturally. It would be fair to say that our first language comes to us almost unconsciously, as a result of natural human interaction.

My second language came with a bit more struggle. It was as if my voice was out of sync with the voices around me—they made sounds, but our sounds did not share the same meaning. If I remember correctly, my brother Alex, who is only eighteen months older than me, said the first word he understood in English was *green*. There is something exhilarating about that moment when a sound takes on a more profound meaning, and something deeply intimate about the moment when two human beings understand each other for the first time. That first stage of connecting language with meaning is no small thing, yet it pales in comparison to the moment when we begin to understand another human being, when another's voice carries meaning. There's often a stage between the ability to understand and the ability to communicate thoughts and feelings. I don't know if there's any feeling more frustrating than desperately wanting to communicate what is inside to another human being while knowing we lack the language to express our deepest thoughts.

However we define mastery of a language, its profound significance is revealed when we progress from knowing the right words to having our own voice, which is the point where we enter into the journey of the artisan soul. Whether we choose to express ourselves through art or literature or struggle to find a career that uniquely expresses who we are and brings us personal happiness, a critical aspect of the journey to express our lives as a creative act is finding our own voice. This seems like an easy part of the process, but it is much harder than we could ever imagine. Like language, our internal voice begins as an echoing of the voices of others. Before we speak for ourselves, others speak on our behalf. Before we are able to declare who we are, our soul forms around the declarations of others telling us who we are.

The soul is that material in us humans that distinguishes us from animals and reflects the divine in us. It is designed to be shaped by our passions, experiences, and values. For whatever reason, the soul is made of malleable material. It forms itself around whatever material is informing it. Unfortunately, the people who have the greatest influence in our lives rarely understand the power of their words to shape who we become. They never fully understand that what informs us forms us. Words spoken into a soul are like the hands of a potter pressed against wet clay.

All too often we use our words carelessly and even at times recklessly. In an ideal world, the voices in our lives place within us the material to become our best selves. The healthiest people I know were raised by parents, families, and communities where the truth was always spoken in love. In an ideal world, the voices that teach us language teach us self-respect, self-confidence, and self-esteem. Those same voices also form in us humility and gratitude, and as those voices inform our inner voices, they also pass on wisdom.

All too often, though, the voices that speak early and deep into our souls are more destructive than constructive. I meet so many people who carry an internal narrative that they have no value and no worth, and are not worthy of love. Some forty-year-old men are still fighting off voices that spoke to them when they were four years old. Over the years, I have come to realize that the crises most people face are less because of their circumstances than because of the narrative inside. Our demons rarely come at us from the future; most often, they chase after us from our past. Far too often, when we think we are frightened by mystery, the fact is that we are haunted by history. This is the tension of the present. There are voices that call us into the future and voices that call us into the past. Eventually, somewhere down the road in the silence of a paralyzing moment, we have to decide what voice will define us and what story we choose to be in—which is the narrative that guides.

To find our own voice, we must first wrestle with the voices inside our brains. Some of those voices could hold us captive the rest of our lives. Some of those voices, if we choose to give them power over us, will make us become less and less as we listen to them more and more. Some voices inside will silence our souls and leave us without a language to express who we really are. To find our own voice, we must be willing to let our souls go silent. Finding our own voice may take the greatest courage we've ever mustered.

There is something comforting about being nothing but an echo. Far too often, we are more afraid of silence than we are of emptiness. If we turn off the volume on all the voices we have become accustomed to, will we have nothing to say? Why would we allow negative, destructive voices to have so much power in our lives unless we had embraced the truth of their words? In the end, all the voices that seek to make us small and irrelevant and worthless find power only when we have allowed them to become our voice. What others think of us, what others have said about us matters, has power, only when it becomes what we think of ourselves and what we say to ourselves about who we are.

Years ago I wrote a poem about this struggle in my own soul. It's entitled "Where the Echoes Stop."

I want to stand where the echoes stop.
Far past where sound has abandoned thought.
Where silence reigns over redundancy.
Where once well said is more than enough.

I want to stand where the echoes stop.
Where words must be born to be heard.
Where speech is a gift and not a curse.
Where there is more of the unique and less of
    the mundane.

I want to stand where the echoes stop.
Where meaning is rescued from noise. . .
Where conviction replaces thoughtless repeti-
    tion. . .
Where what everyone is saying surrenders to
    what needs to be said.

I want to stand where the echoes stop.
Where the shouting of the masses falls silent to
    the whisper of the one. . .
Where the voice of the majority submits to the
    voice of reason. . .
Where "they" do not exist, but "we" do.

I want to stand where the echoes stop.
Where substance overthrows the superficial. . .

Where courage conquers compliance and conformity. . .
Where words do not travel farther than the
person who speaks them.

I want to stand where the echoes stop.
Where I only say what I believe.
Where I only repeat what changes me.
Where empty words finally rest in peace.

I want to stand where the echoes stop.
"Be still and know that I am God" (Psalm 46:10a).

Before we can move forward on this journey of discovering our own voice, we have to choose to stand
where the echoes stop. We also have to believe that
there is a story we are supposed to be in, a story that is
bigger than us and, because of that, a story that makes
us bigger.

At least once a week, a bunch of guys and I take
over an indoor basketball gym and play two hours
of full-court basketball. For two hours, below-average
athletes pretend we are the peers of Chris Paul and
Dwyane Wade. We rarely have a Kevin Garnett, since
most of the guys are no taller than 6'2. Recently,
though, I was playing with a friend on my team who
was 6'6. In our game, he was nothing less than a giant.

Every time I took the ball down, he would set a pick for one of our teammates. The purpose of a pick is to essentially create a wall so that the defender cannot get to you so that you are then either open to shoot or to pass it to the person who set the pick. Each time after setting a pick he was wide open underneath the basket. It was clear to me that easy points were waiting for us, but he never looked up. He would never make eye contact with me. I kept wanting to pass the basketball, and he did everything physically possible to make that impossible.

In the genteel manner I always bring to the game of basketball, I started suggesting that he make eye contact with me. In fact, I began the conversation by calling him out. "I know what you are doing. You are avoiding eye contact. You're avoiding eye contact so I can't pass it to you underneath."

He rose to his defense. "No, I'm setting a pick."

I responded, "I know you are setting a pick. I also know you can make eye contact with me when you are setting a pick. You don't want the ball underneath. You don't think you're open. You're 6'6. With your reach, it makes you 7'6. On this court you are always open. I need you to make eye contact. I know that you're a guard and you're used to playing outside, but somewhere in your life someone told you that you were small and you believed you were small, and now you are playing smaller than you are.

Here you are big. What do I need to do to convince you that you are not small?"

His response caught me off guard. He said, "That's what happens to you when your younger brother is 6'10. You are small, so you learn how to play outside."

It became my goal that day to change his narrative, to replace the internal story that told him he was small with a narrative that made him bigger than life.

I knew exactly what was happening inside my friend—not only because I've seen it so many times in others, but because I have seen it in myself. I have spent my entire life rewriting the story of who I am. The great battles I fought had little to do with the world of others and everything to do with the universe inside me. It was all about disarming the voices that made me less and taking responsibility for my internal narrative. A critical part of this process is listening to the voice that calls me to more. When we win this internal conflict, the battle will be won long before we ever walk on the battlefield.

For several years when I was in the fashion industry, I traveled to New York on a regular basis. One time my family traveled with me, and we spent some time with my former business partner. When you travel as much as I do, you leave remnants of your life everywhere. Unfortunately for me, this has often meant canceling credit cards and securing a new driver's license. I don't know how many wallets I have lost around the world.

Since I was traveling with my family, I wanted to be extra diligent in ensuring that this did not happen on this trip. My wife, Kim, is far less likely to lose things, so I decided to put my wallet in her purse when we took the train to Eastchester. It was a perfect plan until our plans changed. Kim decided to spend the night in Eastchester. My son, Aaron, and I had a meeting in Manhattan the next morning at 7:00 A.M., so we decided to take the train back into the city. When we arrived at the White Plains station, I realized I had left my wallet with Kim, safely tucked inside her purse. Now, to be clear, I didn't lose it—I just forgot it. This was a huge improvement over my previous pattern. (I just didn't want to continue the story without celebrating my progress.)

You can imagine my frustration when I realized I couldn't pay for the train and that I would be cashless the next day in Manhattan. Aaron stepped in to save the day. "Dad, I have my wallet. I've got this. I'll take care of you tomorrow. Nothing to worry about."

I was so proud of him in that moment. His words demonstrated a sense of responsibility he must have learned from his mother. We realized that we had missed the train and that the last train heading back to the city would be over an hour away. We saw a taxi sitting outside. It was dingy, smoke-filled, and cash-only. Aaron and I scraped together all the cash he had and found more than enough money to hire the taxi driver to take us into the city. I needed to go to SoHo, and Aaron was staying in an apartment closer to the U.N., so we decided to have him drop us off at Grand Central Station. From there he could walk to his destination and I could grab the subway to mine.

We decided to be generous with our driver, giving him a gracious tip of every dollar we had. We figured we could rush out of the cab, find an ATM, and get me some cash to make it through the day. Almost like a ballet, we saw an ATM, watched the taxi drive away, and realized that Aaron had left his wallet in the taxi. We were now standing in the middle of Manhattan in the middle of the night without a penny to our names and with zero wallets between us—no credit cards, no ATM cards, no identification, no hope. I might have allowed myself to get frustrated, except that Aaron so quickly became angry at himself. I remember him saying out loud, "I had one task, one job—to take care of you for one night—and I just blew it."

I could feel his frustration and disappointment in himself. I didn't really have a lot of room to talk, since I had left my wallet over an hour away, and I was reminded that my son really is a lot more like me than his mother. It was a beautiful bonding moment through shared weaknesses. We did, of course, still have our cell phones. So I called Kim and explained our dilemma. Without dignifying her response, I will say that she was not helpful. After twenty-nine years of marriage and who knows how many wallets, I have sort of used up all the empathy I'm going to get in this lifetime.

So we began to walk toward SoHo. I suggested he go to his apartment, which was nearby, and allow me to walk, but in his highly protective mode he refused to let me walk the streets of New York on my own in the middle of the night. As we began the two-hour journey, it occurred to me that this was a wonderful teaching moment, but I don't think Aaron would have received it like that.

I said, "Hey, buddy, here's a great opportunity for us to use our problem-solving skills. If we had been dropped off in a foreign city without any resources and/or access to money, how would we solve this problem? What would we do?" We began making phone calls across the country. We called Visa and woke up Alisah Duran, my assistant, in the middle of the night. We had several moments when we thought we had found a solution, followed by moments clarifying that we had not.

Our process was hindered, however, by Aaron's frustration with himself. I could feel his anger and disappointment in himself, along with self-loathing. This is when I began to explain to him the importance of releasing negative emotions and accessing our higher consciousness.

For years I have spent immense energy studying the experience of knowing. I am fascinated by how humans can know things that go beyond facts and information. Other animals know through their senses and perhaps even their instincts. Humans have an uncanny ability to know things they seemingly shouldn't know. We call it intuition or insight, or we attribute it to some kind of mystical capacity. What is clear is that there are individuals who have so developed intelligence beyond mere intellect that their capacity to know appears nearly supernatural.

I began to explain to him that some neuroscientists describe the human brain as divided into three parts, and within that construct we have what is described as a reptilian brain. The idea here is that we humans have an aspect of our mental processes that moves us into our most reptilian expression. This part of our brain involves the aspect of our humanity that deals with aggression, dominance, and self-protection.

This idea was first popularized by neuroscientist Paul D. MacLean. He originally formulated his model in the 1960s and expanded on it in his 1990 book *The Triune Brain in Evolution*. This reptilian complex is incredibly valuable when we're being attacked by a lion, but not that helpful when we are trying to solve complex problems. I told Aaron he needed to let go of his frustration and anger. He needed to clear his mind and move out of his reptilian brain into his intuitive mind.

"Buddy, what I need from you is your highest level of thinking. So I need you to release the part of you that wants to protect and open up the part of you that wants to explore."

He looked at me with curiosity and uncertainty and said, "Okay, Dad. Reptilian brain? I need you to be clear—is this something real or are you making it up?"

I am absolutely certain that my son would tell you that I am the most truthful person he knows, but that question does not come without context. When he was a little boy, I once told him I was an alien from another planet and showed him the alien registration card that I received when I immigrated to the United States of America. I thought he was going to have a heart attack back then. As much as I enjoy a great joke, it clearly left a permanent scar.

I laughed and assured him that I was not making this up. This was an actual theory. He could check Wikipedia and it would be there. Even if this new understanding of how the human mind works did not exist, the truth of it still resonates with the Scriptures. There may be no better description of this dynamic tension than that found in the book of Psalms. When describing the effect of setting free the captives of

Israel, Psalm 126:1–2 says, "We were like those who dreamed. Our mouths were filled with laughter, our tongues with songs of joy." When captives are freed, there is a substantive change in their mindsets. They are like men who dream, and because they are like men who dream, their mouths are filled with laughter and their tongues with songs of joy.

There is a direct relationship between those who live most free and those who dream most. Captivity not only steals our freedom but cripples our imagination. Slavery crushes the divine narrative within us and seeks to replace it with another narrative to convince us that we are less than those who hold us captive. When the captives were released, they were not only freed from their oppressors but they were free to dream again.

One of the unexpected discoveries during my ten years of working with the urban poor was how poverty changes a person. Not always but far too often, physical poverty drives us to a poverty of the soul. I knew when I walked into a world of impoverishment that I would meet people who lacked food and shelter and education. I knew that I would spend my days with individuals and families who had been deprived of their basic human needs. I knew that centuries of oppression and injustice had robbed them of much of their dignity, opportunity, and freedom. What I didn't know was that the weight of poverty had stolen from most of them their capacity to imagine a life better than the one they had always known.

I quickly realized that it was essential for me to do the basic work of helping people solve the real problems of their daily struggle. I needed to help them find a place to live, a job that would pay their bills, and the skills necessary for a better life. But most important, it was critical that I somehow find a way to help these individuals, whom I had come to care so much about, learn to dream again. People only become slaves when they have lost their dreams. I am certain that every master knows this. You may have people in chains, but you don't own them until you have stolen their souls. If they dream of freedom, your power over them is an illusion. Even Paul makes this nuanced distinction in his letter to the Galatians, when he says that even if the son is an heir, as long as he is a child, he still lives like a slave. Until the voice that guides us declares our freedom, nothing and no one in the world can make us free. As long as the voice that defines who we are declares our freedom, no one and nothing can hold us captive. Which leads to the critical question: What is the narrative that guides us?

I imagine most of us are familiar with the opening chapter of the human story in Genesis. To make sure we are all up to speed, in the opening scene we find God creating man. This was the beginning of the first conversation. God brings Adam into the creative process, inviting him to name every animal on the face of the earth. It simply tells us that whatever the man named them, that's what they were called. What an exhilarating moment, for man to walk side by side with God and know that his voice was heard, that what he said mattered and in fact defined reality.

Then we are told that God saw it was not good for man to be alone, so he put the man into a deep sleep and created woman. Have you ever been in such an extraordinary place that you thought to yourself, it can't get better than this? That's what Adam's life was like just before he went to sleep. It can't get any better than this—or can it? Quickly Adam discovered that, yes, it can. He awoke to Eve, and the world that was already paradise became better still. I love how God meets a need that Adam had no language for. It is a beautiful picture of the intimate concern of God.

But as we know, the story continues and a serpent enters the scene. And this manifestation of evil introduces a new narrative. God has been very clear: "You are free to eat from any tree in the garden; but you must not eat from the tree of the knowledge of good and evil, for when you eat from it you will certainly die" (Genesis 2:16–17).

The serpent, of course, questions the truth of God's story. He becomes a conflicting voice. He convinces the woman and the man that God is not telling them the whole story, that the voice of God is not the one who would guide them to life—that he is, in fact, holding out on them, keeping the best for himself. Adam and Eve silence the voice of God and choose a lesser narrative for themselves. The moment they eat the fruit of this tree, they find themselves in a painfully dark story. And as it always happens, company arrives when you least want it—God shows up on the scene. Aside from everything else that is about to happen, I love the question God asks the man: "Who told you that you were naked?" Whose voice did you replace my voice with? What story did you embrace? Who gave you this new narrative that now guides you and leaves you empty?

When I was about ten years old I had the bad habit of forgetting my towel when I would shower. I will never forget one occasion when after asking for a towel my shower was suddenly interrupted by two family members who broke into the bathroom and dragged me out of the shower naked. They proceeded to throw me out of the house, locking me outside for the world to see. All I could think to do, after my pleas to let me in went unanswered, was to run and hide behind a bush. It was a bare bush with nowhere near the amount of leaves necessary for cover.

I remember cars driving by and people on bikes going by slowly pointing in my direction. I was humiliated and ashamed. I don't know why I was ashamed or who told me I should be. It was instinctive.

It makes me think of the woman caught in the act of adultery, brought naked before Jesus, cowering in her shame. They wished to trap Jesus and stone the woman at the same time. He lays out a piercing gauntlet to those eager for "justice."

"If any of you is without sin, let him be the first to throw a stone at her." Easy enough, right? One by one, from oldest to youngest, they dropped their stones and their accusations. After Jesus drove away all who would have her stoned to death, he simply asks her, "Has no one condemned you?"

"No one," she answers.

"Then neither do I condemn you. Go now and leave your life of sin" (John 8:7–11).

I'm struck that Jesus never mentions her nakedness. Neither does he move to having someone cover her. It's almost as if he never sees her nakedness. I began to wonder if the woman who was dragged there in her shame was strangely able to walk home naked, free from the shame that had previously covered her. Is it possible to be naked and unashamed?

It made me think of David when he was king of Israel returning from battle. We are told that he danced naked before the Lord as he worshiped, to give God thanks for all of His goodness. David's wife was livid (I empathize with her) that he had humiliated himself before the servant girls and, of course, his wife.

He responded, "I will become even more undignified than this" (2 Samuel 6:22). This was his declaration that he fully intended to live a life of shameless love for God. David knew his voice. He knew his story. He knew the narrative that guided his life. For him it all began with the voice of God who had spoken deep within his soul.

Looking back I wish I had handled my dilemma differently. I wish that when they dragged me outside in my nakedness I had realized it wasn't my shame to bear. I wish I had instead danced in my birthday suit until my heart knew only joy. I wish I had known how to dance like David did. I wish I had heard the voice of the one who speaks into our nakedness and teaches us to dance naked in the rain. Somebody told us we were naked and that we should be ashamed. Ever since we have lived in fear of being our true selves and have remained hidden. We live hidden from ourselves, from one another, and from the God who made us.

He sees us not in our nakedness but in our shame. He comes to free us from the fear of being truly and fully seen. To find our voice we must stand naked and unashamed.

This is the question God asks us all: Who told you that you were naked? Who have you been listening to? Who has led you to where you are right now? What voice did you embrace? What story corrupted your soul? Why would you choose a narrative that only leads you to death?

This is a tragic reminder that we humans have the strange capacity to live a soulless life. Our inner voice was never supposed to be simply an echo; our inner voice was always to resonate with the voice of God. Every other voice will either make us less than we were intended to be or convince us that we are more than we really are. Neither self-loathing nor self-worship helps us find our authentic voice. It is only when our inner voice responds to the voice of God that we begin to truly find our own voice.

As critical as it is for us to understand that art is always an extension of ourselves, the creative act is also an expression of our essence. It is equally important for us to realize that our guiding narrative determines the story we tell through our lives. Our inner voice not only informs us of who we are but affects everything we touch and in the end becomes the driving force through which we strive to shape the world around us. The principal creative act, described in Genesis 1, begins with God speaking the universe into existence. God speaks out of who he is, and everything in creation is a declaration of his glory and an expression of his personhood.

The Scriptures remind us over and over of the

power of the spoken word. The story of all humanity came into being from the voice of God. He is the master storyteller. He was always intended to give to us the narrative that guides. The voice that spoke light into existence is the one we need to expel the darkness within and bring us to light, to life, and to love. Working on us like an instrument that is out of tune, God masterfully tightens and loosens the strings until the notes resonate properly and reflect the most beautiful of sounds. We find our voice when we find his voice. It's here that we experience our most authentic selves and find our true voice. In the end every artist creates only art that reflects the inner voice.

Years ago, I spent an entire semester studying the work of Vincent van Gogh. His is a tragic story filled with extreme beauty and overwhelming sorrow. His paintings reflect the tormented soul of a man whose dark imagination weighed more heavily than his hope. The progression of his work is a direct reflection of his aspirations, his struggles, and eventually, his tormented inner world. His artistic genius is undeniable, which allows us to glean a keen insight into the struggle we all have within us. Even when there is talent, there is always self-doubt and inner uncertainties.

Van Gogh once wrote, "If you hear a voice within you say 'you cannot paint,' then by all means paint and that voice will be silenced."

You can replace the word *paint* with any dream we might pursue. There will always be conflicting voices within us—those that whisper about the great dreams waiting to be realized and those that scream that we lack the talent or capacity to achieve them. Part of that process is deciding which voices will inform us. I love how Claude Monet, a French impressionist who brought us an entirely new way of seeing reality, literally turned his back on the Louvre to put his focus on nature. During his early years in Paris, while other painters would go to the Louvre to imitate the paintings of the greats who had found their way into this gallery, Monet would go to the window and begin to paint what he saw outside. Monet's internal narrative was deeply rooted in the wonder and beauty of nature. He brought with his perceptions an astonishing use of color and movement.

Monet was mesmerized by the beauty around him. His work is the expression of a man drowning in a universe of overwhelming beauty. He saw the beautiful everywhere. He once wrote in his journal, "Every day I discover more and more beautiful things. It is enough to drive one mad."

While van Gogh's narrative was a journey of inner turmoil, Monet became a translator of beauty. In both artists, we can easily see how the internal narrative directly informs the process of the creative act. It is easy enough to see the connection between our inner voice and how that translates not only in the creation of art, but more importantly when we realize that our lives are our most significant works of art.

Perhaps the most poignant example of an artist whose inner voice shaped his outer world was Pablo Picasso. Picasso is one of the best-known figures of the twentieth century and arguably the most influential artist of that era. Picasso's art was more than groundbreaking; it was revolutionary. His extraordinary talent was matched only by his fearless exploration and extraordinary creativity.

More fascinating than his view of art was his view of humanity. In an era when no one held such a high view of the creative nature of each person, Picasso wrote, "Every child is an artist. The problem is how to remain an artist once we grow up." He confounds expectation when he says, "It took me four years to paint like Raphael, but a lifetime to paint like a child."

Picasso understood that the artist is also a work of art, that the one who creates is also in a sense being created. He makes clear in his description of the artistic journey that we are being informed and formed long before we begin to express ourselves as artists and creators: "The artist is a receptacle of emotions that come from all over the place—from the sky, from the earth, from a scrap of paper, from a passing shape, from a spider's web."

Picasso's narrative is characterized by a drive for human uniqueness and a strong sense of his own personal genius. One of Picasso's earliest memories is the internal narrative passed on to him by his mother. "My mother said to me 'If you are a soldier, you will become a general. If you are a monk, you will become the Pope.' Instead, I was a painter and became Picasso."

Could there be a clearer connection between a person's internal narrative and the expression of his life as a creative act? Pablo had nowhere else he could go, no one else he could become but Picasso.

My mind begins to reel when imagining what this world would look like if all of us believed our lives could become masterpieces. What would the world be like if each of us had an inner voice that awakened within us our greatest self? I am reminded of those moments in biblical history when unique individuals suddenly hear the voice of God, that moment when they are undeniably called out to live a life bigger than themselves.

Quite often God marries that encounter with a new name. Abram becomes Abraham; Sarai becomes Sarah; Jacob (which means deceiver) becomes Israel; Simon becomes Peter; and Saul becomes Paul. I suppose the only question that remains is: Who do we become when we stop allowing all the voices in our head to crowd out the one voice we must hear to come to life?

I have joked on occasion that the difference between a sane man and an insane one is that the sane man can identify all the voices in his head and the insane man thinks all those voices are his. Whether we realize it or not, our souls are overcrowded with voices demanding attention—more than that, demanding allegiance, adherence, submission. If we're not careful, we will live our lives as echoes, an imitation of our authentic selves. When we hear the voice of God or heed Jesus's invitation to follow him, it leads us out of captivity into freedom. When we hear God's voice, we finally find our voice. When we find our voice, we discover we finally have something to say, and that when we speak, our words have power. We bring voice to the hopes that have long been lost to a world trapped in a noisy silence.

This morning, before I began this chapter, I was thinking that when we find our authentic voices, we discover our authentic selves and begin to live our most authentic lives. I reflected on how we mirror the nature of God. I thought to myself that through the Word of God all things good are created. The power of this voice is our way to freedom. As I reflected on the narrative that guides, Aaron sent me a note from New York with no explanation, only these words: "His words spoken into existence alter humanity forever."

That in a nutshell is exactly what this chapter is about. "The Word became flesh and made his dwelling among us. We have seen his glory, the glory of the one and only Son, who came from the Father, full of grace and truth" (John 1:14). When God speaks, life happens.

2012 will go down for me as one of the most difficult and painful years of my life. It will also always be the marker of the beginning of a better and more beautiful future.

I was a successful entrepreneur in the world of fashion and film, art and story, committed to building a brand that would influence faith and culture for generations. Adding to that the opportunity to work as a futurist and thought leader in multiple domains allowed me access and influence to a broader world than ever before.

Kim and I were able to be so generous in a season of great success and wealth. We built homes for the homeless, dug wells in Africa, helped young girls find freedom from the sex trade, literally helped orphans and widows in need, and were able to invest deeply in the work of Mosaic as it reached Los Angeles and touched the world.

I was on an amazing journey weaving together

spirituality and creativity. It was all about beauty, story, and meaning. Clearly this was the life I was meant to live. I was living the dream.

It became a nightmare.

I woke up one day to a painful betrayal where I saw years of work and millions of dollars lost. A future I thought was certain was lost in a moment, and my life felt like it had been turned into rubble. My dreams and hopes turned to ashes and dust.

I had to fly home and tell my wife Kim that I lost everything. I was devastated. I couldn't eat or sleep. I lost twenty pounds from stress (which looking back worked out well for me). More than once I felt as if I would simply fall into the fetal position and stay there for life. Some days all I could do was breathe.

Feeling such deep loss and an overwhelming sense of failure I was reminded of the words of a dear friend of mine, Mako Fujimura. At the beginning of this venture I understood the risks involved in such a huge undertaking. I shared with Mako that I didn't know if I would succeed, but I knew it was worth the risk.

Without hesitation he looked me dead in the eyes and said with absolute certainty, "You have already succeeded." I asked him why he would say that and his response was just as sure. "Because you have a story to tell. You have a story worth telling, and because of that the outcome is irrelevant to your success."

I never forgot those words. They mattered then, but they matter so much more now.

Our story is what we have to offer the world. So much more important than being heard is having something to say. Without a voice our words are just sounds. I wish I had a different story than the one I just lived through, but I am so grateful for the story that has made me who I am today.

Even the pain. Even the wounds.

The sadness was real.

The brokenness deep.

The scars mine.

It's my story.

It's who I am.

It's how I'm becoming.

Artists are not only great storytellers; their lives tell a great story. In them the word becomes flesh. They hear the voice that calls them to their destiny.

When God speaks universes are created.

What is His voice creating within you?

Interpretation

Translation of Life

Over the years, I've been asked quite often who my favorite communicators are. Although I know exactly what the questioner means, I always answer by naming a film director. There are an endless number of great speakers that I admire and appreciate deeply, but it is inescapable that the best storytellers of our time are filmmakers. Who tells a better story than Steven Spielberg or Ridley Scott or Kathryn Bigelow? That's without even mentioning Christopher Nolan or Quentin Tarantino.

One of my personal favorites, though, is Terrence Malick. I am intrigued both by the stories he chooses to tell and by how he tells the stories. In 2011, I was invited to be on a panel at one of the preview events for Malick's *The Tree of Life*. The theater was filled with connectors and influencers from every field of religious and philosophical thought. If I remember correctly, the panel consisted of a Jewish rabbi, a Muslim man, a Catholic nun, an Evangelical pastor, a film critic, an atheist, and me. I'm not really sure which demographic I was invited to represent. One of the unique aspects of a Malick film is how wonderfully obscure they are. His films are more aptly described as visual poetry than simply narrative storytelling. So one of the central questions in the Q&A after the film was, what in the world does this movie mean? It's rare to see a movie with Brad Pitt, Sean Penn, Jessica Chastain, and dinosaurs.

The title clearly invites us to grapple with the deepest questions of human existence: Why are we here? Does life have any meaning? The film even presses deeply into the role and place of God in the story of man. During most of the Q&A, I found myself enjoying listening from the stage. The questions and insights were so varied. It was fascinating.

Eventually, though, I was pressed to express my thoughts on Malick's meaning. What was my interpretation? What stood out to me was a scene that could be perceived as innocuous or even irrelevant to the whole, but which struck me as the central metaphor of the film.

Brad Pitt plays an old-school Texas father whose relationship to his family is cold and distant. I imagine that if interviewed, his family would describe their relationship more in terms of fear and respect than love and admiration. In this scene, we find Brad Pitt's character sitting in his chair with a lighter on the table to his right, clearly within reach. He grabs his cigarette, but then we see his son walk briskly past him. He abruptly asks his son to come and hand him his lighter. There is an awkward pause during which his son seems to hesitate, then moves toward his father and picks up the lighter. He hands it to his father without saying a word and quickly turns to go back the way he came.

Brad Pitt's character abruptly asks, "Didn't you forget something?" and the son hesitantly returns and kisses his father on the face. Then Brad Pitt's character asks him, "Do you love your father?"—the kind of question that if you have to ask, the answer is clear. But his son, out of fear, answers with a yes, more as a means of escape than an attempt to find an emotional bond with his father.

This scene illustrates the central human dilemma in our search for God. God is seen as a cruel taskmaster—cold, aloof, and indifferent. Our only interactions with him occur when he arbitrarily invades our lives and commands us to do his bidding while he sits idly by and watches us work. At the same time, it seemed like Brad Pitt's character's awkward attempt to draw his son closer. He obviously could get his own lighter. He was a hardworking man and clearly wasn't so lazy that he couldn't lean over half a foot. By calling his son over to grab his lighter, he was in his own awkward and sublime way inviting his son to come near. It wasn't the lighter he wanted; it was the kiss. And it wasn't the kiss that was his ultimate desire; it was the affection of his son.

I wonder if this is the difference between religion and worship. Religion is our response to God from a perspective of coercion and compliance. We fear God, so we do his bidding and risk coming near him, all the while waiting to put distance between ourselves and our Creator. God is, however, profoundly misunderstood. Worship is not something we are called to so that God can reinforce his status. It is his way of calling us near. He asks us to grab the lighter and set the altar on fire—not because he could not do it himself, but because he wants us to come near. He wants us to realize that while we thought all he wanted from us was the work, it was actually an invitation to come near and know his love.

You could imagine my surprise when *The Wall Street Journal* picked up this story and spread it across the country. Frankly, it's somewhat ironic, since I have no idea if this is what Terrence Malick meant at all. It was just my interpretation, my translation, of his story. I have to wonder, though, if this wasn't Malick's artistic intent and if he perhaps tells a story in such a way that we do not simply hear his interpretation of the human story but begin to discover our own interpretation of the meaning of everything. *The Tree of Life* is either filled with contradictions and seemingly disconnected narratives or it is filled with windows into the human soul.

Films like *The Tree of Life*, *Life of Pi*, and even *Avatar* force us to face an important insight about human nature: truth is not nearly as powerful as interpretation. I hope you bristled when you read that line. I bristled when I wrote it. I want us to take a deep breath and exhale, to notice that my statement works from the assumption of truth. I resolved a long time ago that truth exists only if there is someone who is trustworthy. The truth is an extension of someone who can be trusted. The truth exists because God is trustworthy. There is a truth upon which we can build our lives, but that truth, contrary to how our modern minds want to work, is not about data. Truth is not a piece of information but a person. Jesus said it simply: "I am the truth." I have become convinced over a lifetime that the human spirit lives in the fullness for which we are created only when we live in truth. The farther we move from truth, the more un-healthy we become. The more we live in truth, the more we find wholeness and become our most authentic selves.

That said, I still hold to my earlier statement—interpretation is more important than truth in that all truth, all human experience, every narrative and every story, in the end changes us only after we have engaged it and interpreted it through our own story. Truth finds its way into the inner recesses of our soul only through interpretation. In the end, only we can decide if another person's story will cause us to believe in God. In the end, we decide which story becomes our story.

We are interpreters. This is the way we are designed. We are translators of meaning, and thus everything we see, hear, smell, touch, taste, and experience is processed through all our previous experiences and perceptions. We don't see people for who they are; we see them through the filter of everyone we've ever known. We don't see circumstances as they are; we see them through the filter of everything we've ever experienced. No experience is an experience in isolation. Every experience is interpreted by the overarching story of our lives, and those experiences give us greater clarity.

Art is an interpretation of life. At its essence, reduced to its most simple expression, art is our translation of all human experience. More than that, it is the artist's personal interpretation of their experience of life. Art is an expression of our emotions; art is an interpretation of our experiences; art in its highest form is a mirror of life. If life is a work of art and life is to become our most creative act, then we must realize that our lives will be our most profound interpretation of what it truly means to be human. Through our lives, we paint a picture of what we believe and what we have experienced.

Have you ever noticed how many artists are informed by the darkest and most painful human experiences? I find the overwhelming majority see tragedy, suffering, and pain as essential to their creative process. I would go as far as to say that many, if not most, feel it is impossible to create when life is going well. I remember once hearing my daughter, Mariah, who is an incredibly talented singer and songwriter, explain that she simply couldn't write because she was too happy. She mused that she might need to break up with her boyfriend to be able to get back to work. I tried to convince her that you never need to hurry pain along. Pain and suffering will find you soon enough.

The creative process is far too often inspired by our most painful experiences rather than our most inspiring ones. It would not be a stretch to say that for many artists, authenticity and tragedy are inseparable. The darker you are, the more honest you are. If you are hopeful, it means you haven't fully embraced your humanity. Optimism is superficial; despair is what honesty looks like.

For years I wondered why it was that even I found darkness a more powerful creative space than light. Why was it that I was somehow more inspired to write, to create, to take time to express my deepest human longings when my soul felt empty, hollow, and estranged? I have come to realize that if the artistic process demands anything from us, it is that the artist must always tell the truth. For the academic, truth can be an objective reality observed and examined. For the artist, truth must be more than that. Something isn't true unless it is both experienced and profoundly subjective. Only that which changes us is true to us; that is the mantra of the true artist. This can be the material for both an ever-expanding universe of creativity and the paralyzing limitation of subjectivity. This relationship to truth often leaves us too little space to travel. If we travel alone, all we know to tell is the story of our profound aloneness. If all we've known is pain and we can only create out of what we know, then this is all the material available to us.

I remember when Mariah was fourteen. She wrote a song that would be used years later in the season finale of *Grey's Anatomy*. One line stood out to me from the very beginning: "Give me a match and I'll burn it all down." You can only imagine how Kim and I felt as Mariah sang her song to us in the living room, a song filled with so much pain, despair, and anger. I think Kim felt a bit betrayed. We had tried so hard to be good parents. I felt really confused. Mariah seemed like such a happy child. In fact, I had described her as sunshine wrapped up in skin.

So after she finished her beautiful piece, not wanting in any way to discourage her authentic expression of her story, I asked her, "Mariah, we've always loved you. It seems like you have had a really beautiful life. Where did that come from? There's so much pain in that song."

She smiled from ear to ear, beaming as she always does. She said, "Oh, I'm not writing for myself. I'm writing for the pain of others."

It struck me that this, too, is part of the artistic journey. The role of the artist is partly to interpret the human story. They in a sense write for all of us. That's why millions of teenage girls buy music by Taylor Swift, Kelly Clarkson, and Adele. They are writing for all teenage girls.

A significant part of the artistic challenge is to go beyond interpreting human experience to be an interpreter of human possibility. It is so much easier to create an authentic work of art informed by despair, so much more difficult to create a true masterpiece informed by optimism and hope. Yet these are the most compelling people—the ones who have overcome tragedy and found beauty; the ones who should have drowned in despair but found hope; the ones who should have forever remained trapped in this rubble of their failures and yet found courage and resolve to rise from the dead.

In life I have found two kinds of people to be the most uninteresting. (Is it okay to admit that there are people who are uninteresting?) The first is the person who has never suffered. It is still surprising to me, but I have met people who told me that they have never suffered, they have never failed; they have lived a life absolutely devoid of pain and disappointment. Living as long as I have, I have discovered that people who live these Teflon lives have only managed that outcome by living a life without risk, courage, passion, or love. We cannot love deeply or risk greatly and never know failure or disappointment. Not even God was able to pull that one off. Love never comes without wounds; faith never comes without failure.

But there is another kind of uninteresting person. It is the person who has suffered, and that suffering is all they know. They are trapped in their pain; they wallow in their despair; they are all wounds and no scars. All they can talk about is their pain. Life is suffering, and the suffering does not make them empathetic. They have no room for the pain of others. Their pain fills their entire universe. They are not interested in your story; they are not interested in your wounds; they are not interested in your pain. They are interested in you only if you are interested in them. They become emotional transients, nomadic wanderers moving from one person to another as each person unwittingly feeds their self-absorption, at first not realizing they do not want to find a way through their pain but only to trap others in their own endless suffering. As uninteresting as the person who has never suffered may be, this person wins the prize. It's hard to tell a great story if we remain stuck in chapter one.

Beyond despair there must always be hope; beyond betrayal there must be a story of forgiveness; beyond failure there must be a story of resilience. If the story ended at the cross, it might be a story worth telling, but that story could never give life. Only the Resurrection makes the Crucifixion what it is for all of us who are marked by the cross.

The life of Jesus should be a compelling narrative to everyone who longs to live the life of a true artisan. Choosing to live simply, he lived humanity's most profound life. Two thousand years later, the life of Jesus remains the world's most powerful message and metaphor. He was both interpreter of God and interpreter of man. Through his life, we have come to understand who God is as well as who we were always intended to be. The last hours of his life have become known around the world as the Passion, which is a beautiful reminder to us all that receiving finds its beauty only when there is meaning and intention. To those who watched his life, he said simply, "If you really know me, you will know my Father as well" (John 14:7). For those of us who have been changed by his life, we understand that in him we find the promise of who we can become.

In the same way, each of us is a translator of life. Our lives are to be an interpretation of our experience with God and an expression of what it means to be fully human. This is no small challenge. We live in the crucible between the promise of who we can become and the reality of who we have been. We exist between tragedy and triumph, failure and success, life and death, hate and love, and this in-between can be like an abyss where we feel lost and torn. It is here, though, in this tension that we find the most interesting people. These are not the watchers who never risk stepping outside the confines of their own safety to experience life at its fullest, nor are they wallowers trapped in a quagmire of suffering. Instead they are artisans who refuse to embrace life as anything less than the greatest work of art.

I have worked with interpreters before. It is an interesting experience to speak in English and hear your words immediately translated into German or Korean or Japanese. It's hard to explain, but even when you don't understand a language, you have a keen sense of whether the translator is expressing your thoughts accurately and authentically.

I remember in Germany once stopping the interpreter in the middle of my talk and challenging him in front of the thousands in the audience. I was certain that he not only had not translated what I said but had in fact reinterpreted my words and said quite the opposite. So I stopped, stepped into this uncomfortable moment, and asked him a simple question. It was really more of a statement. "You didn't say what I said, did you? In fact, you said the opposite of what I said. You just said what you thought I should say, but not what I did say."

After a long pause, he acknowledged that I was exactly right. Afterward, he asked me onstage, "How did you know that?"

I'm not completely sure how I knew. But I do know that I have a pretty good sense of how an audience will respond when a certain statement is made. The statement I made was somewhat controversial. The response of the audience was immediate and willing adherence. I knew that thousands of Germans would not respond in such a positive way to what I had just said. Interpretation is far more than language; inter-

pretation goes to essence. Interpretation is the translation of the soul.

Have you ever met someone who told you everything that was true about God but did not resonate
with the essence of God? It's no small thing to hear
that God is love, but hearing that truth is not nearly
as powerful as experiencing that love from another
human being. When truth is used as a tool for con-
demnation and judgment, it's hard to understand the
words of Jesus: "You will know the truth, and the truth
will set you free" (John 8:32). Remember, the artisan
soul finds truth in essence, not in information. It is
who we are that is the material for our greatest work
of art. From that essence we begin to discover our
own voice, and that inner voice is the declaration of
our authentic story.

In finding our voice, we must pay careful attention to the interpretation of the story we are in. As
storytellers, we find meaning in all of life's experiences and also bring meaning to the lives of others.
Our great fear is that we will never live a life worth
sharing with others, never live a story worth telling,
but that we will find ourselves trapped in a story for
which there is no ending, only an endless cycle of
disappointment and defeat. The lie that paralyzes us
is that those failures and disappointments disqualify
us from living out the great story of our lives. The

reality is that our struggles and suffering give us the context to tell the greatest story of our lives. To do this, though, we must discover the unique characteristics that distinguish those individuals who have known both tragedy and triumph, who have found the dancing after the mourning, and who have learned to count it all joy when they faced trials of many kinds.

Years ago I had the privilege of hearing Daniel Kahneman while participating in a community known as TED, for technology, entertainment, and design. He is widely regarded as the world's most influential living psychologist, and he won a Nobel Prize for his pioneering work on economic behavior. In one presentation, he talked about how we are all essentially two selves—our experienced self and our remembered self—and how in essence we do not choose between experiences, but rather between memories of experiences. According to Kahneman, even when we think about the future, we think of our future not as experiences but as anticipated memories.

What struck me in his observation of our two selves is the idea that our personal happiness is rooted not in our experienced self but in our remembered self. In fact, in some strange way our experiences have a minimal effect on our personal happiness. This is not to say that we do not have painful experiences that bring us great sorrow. But in the end our experiences are not the dominant force affecting our personal happiness. It is instead our remembered self that controls how we perceive and experience life.

You and I have both met people who have gone through real pain and suffering in their lives that they struggled to get past. I know in my life I have met many such people. I find it difficult to see how they could overcome such tragedy. Sometimes life comes with such blunt force trauma that the natural and human response is to curl up in a fetal position and hope that somehow the world will just go away. Yet inevitably we soon meet someone else who has suffered just as deeply and yet that person has some-how risen above their pain. They remember the pain but are no longer trapped in it. Occasionally we have the privilege of meeting that rare individual whose story is filled with such overwhelming tragedy that we wonder how in the world they can see so much beauty all around them. Yet those people do exist— people who have suffered more than you or me and yet remain more hopeful, more optimistic, and yes, even more joyful and happy.

Kahneman is saying that it is not our experiences but how we remember those experiences and even what experiences we choose to remember that have the most profound effect on our happiness. I see this in its extremes all the time. Frankly, the people who whine the most about how hard their lives are have very rarely experienced much to be disappointed about. They seem to find solace in their most negative memories, using these as a blank check that abdicates them from all personal responsibility. "I am how I am because of the pain of my past. If you had experienced what I have experienced, you would understand my bitterness, my anger, my paralysis, my despair."

Perhaps the reason I found Kahneman's observations so compelling is that over a decade ago I wrote a book called *Uprising,* where I had made similar observations without the scientific or empirical data. Some of my conclusions were very personal. I remembered being shaped as a young boy by five or six of my most negative experiences. I relived those experiences over and over again. In fact, I can safely say that it was not those experiences but my decision to live in those experiences every day for the rest of my life that put me in psychiatric care by the time I was twelve and in and out of the hospital for psychosomatic disorders. As bad as my experiences may have been, other people have experienced far worse. I simply chose to be defined by my worst experiences and crafted my remembered self around them.

Somehow, around the age of thirteen I made a conscious decision to relinquish those memories as the material with which I defined my life. I could not

change my experiences—what happened, happened—
but I could change my focus and my interpretation.
I began consciously rewriting my personal history,
determined to learn from my most negative experiences and use them as the material to develop my
best self. I also was determined to remember the best
experiences ever given to me as a gift in my childhood. I cannot understate the power of this process.
It not only changed how I remembered my childhood, but it changed me.

I know without any doubt that our experiences are
not nearly as powerful as our memories. We must
never allow ourselves to believe that we are the sum
total of our experiences. Though our experiences
are real, we are more than those experiences. The
moment we define ourselves by our experiences, we
have lost our way. Be informed by your experiences
but do not be controlled by them.

What has happened to us is not nearly as powerful or as formative as our interpretation of why it
happened. Our most destructive emotions, such as
bitterness and unforgivingness, root deeply into the
human soul not because of what happened to us
but because we haven't resolved the issues of why.
Why would someone hurt you? Why would someone
betray you? Why would God allow this? Why did this
happen to me? This is where interpretation becomes
humanity's most powerful agent.

Your remembered self is your translation of life. It is the *why* to all the *what*. Interpretation is a form of selective memory. Because of the way the human brain is designed, when we remember a past experience we are actually reliving it. Our brains seem incapable of distinguishing the actual event from the remembered event. Within the construct of the human brain, the experience and the memory are one and the same.

Why in the world would we want to relive our worst moment a thousand times? We're not just reopening a wound; we're allowing ourselves to be wounded over and over. If forgiveness has no other value, it at least ends any control the other party has over our life. The unforgiven remain free to own us, to hurt us, to define us. We are never fully free until we have fully forgiven.

To engage our lives as a creative act, we must understand that a significant part of the creative process is interpretation. Our interpretation of life determines the material from which we will build the future. The great danger, of course, is that who we are and who we are meant to be can so easily be lost in translation.

One of the best examples of interpretation is the book of Job. I love how Job is written as a Greek tragedy: forty-plus chapters to bring us to one realization. The book begins with a conversation between

God and Satan about the life of this man Job. The question posed to God by his nemesis is: Would Job still worship you if you were not so good to him?

It's an important question. Is God worthy of our lives only if he brings us effortless success? So in the story God allows Satan to take from Job everything that brings him joy, but he is not allowed to end Job's life. He can, however, make Job wish he were dead. As the story progresses, three friends come to interpret Job's experiences: Eliphaz the Temanite, Bildad the Shuhite, and Zophar the Naamathite. The Bible tells us they came to sympathize and comfort him. At first they don't speak a word when they see how great Job's suffering is, but it doesn't take them long to become the interpreters of his story. One by one they make their best effort to craft what could be best described as Job's remembered self. They take his experiences and attribute their own meaning to them, each in their own way condemning Job and using his experiences to prove he is not the man they once thought he was.

It would be an understatement to say that Job's story didn't make sense even to himself. If we take the story at face value, Job was not being punished for anything he did wrong. If anything, Job had garnered the admiration and affection of God himself. Job was the best example of a life well lived. There's nothing more confusing than to live a life pursuing

God's highest ideals and then watch your life fall prey to unspeakable tragedy. Each of Job's friends was essentially answering the question "Why?" in an attempt to understand what had happened. Eventually Job, too, struggled with the why. Our great temptation in times like this is to assume the worst of ourselves, to assume the worst of others, and in the end to even assume the worst of God. That's why the resolution of Job 42, chapters later, is such a beautiful and compelling moment. Job's response to God has a powerful humility to it: "Surely I spoke of things I did not understand, things too wonderful for me to know. You said, 'Listen now and I will speak; I will question you, and you shall answer me.' My ears had heard of you but now my eyes have seen you. Therefore I despise myself and repent in dust and ashes" (Job 42:3–6).

I love the fact that God has an epilogue to the story. He goes to Job's three friends (with friends like this, who needs enemies?), and says to them, "I am angry with you and your two friends, because you have not spoken the truth about me, as my servant Job has. So now take seven bulls and seven rams and go to my servant Job and sacrifice a burnt offering for yourselves. My servant Job will pray for you, and I will accept his prayer and not deal with you according to your folly. You have not spoken the truth about me, as my servant Job has" (Job 42:7–8).

You know the end of the story: God blesses Job in the latter part of his life even more than he did in the first, restoring to him sons and daughters and great wealth and prosperity.

The power of the story of Job is in Job's struggle, through multiple interpretations of his life, to discover and embrace the true meaning of his suffering. I love how the book of Job addresses through its literary form the destructive power as well as the significance of our interpretation of human experiences. Interpretation is the means by which we bring meaning to our experiences. As people of faith, who live our lives in the truth of the Scripture, we understand the importance of interpretation. Rarely do we think about the importance of the interpretation of life. We see life through a filter. That filter either blinds us to all the beauty, wonder, and possibility that surrounds us, or it brings them to light.

Our interpretation will be informed either by the worst of who we can be or by the best of what it means to be human. When we allow our filter to be shaped by bitterness and jealousy and envy and greed and hatred and apathy, our interpretation of life is skewed and the future becomes smaller and smaller. It is here that our interpretation of life causes us to experience each day with doubt and apprehension. When our interpretation of life is informed by the best of human emotions, when we are informed by love and hope and faith, it changes the way we see everything.

It was Einstein who said, "There are two ways to live your life—one is as though nothing is a miracle and the other is as if everything is a miracle." Interpretation matters. What is your interpretation of life?

Image

Manifestation of Imagination

One of my favorite scenes in the movie *Hook* is when Peter Pan was first brought to Neverland and invited to a banquet. All the Lost Boys sat at a grand table, drooling in anticipation of the feast they were about to enjoy. One by one, they began to devour an endless supply of the most delicious food a human being could ever imagine. Everyone was enjoying the feast except Peter Pan. From his vantage point, there was nothing there—the table was empty. The Lost Boys had lost their minds. If they

92 ERWIN RAPHAEL MCMANUS

were eating an impossibly delicious meal, it was for that exact reason—the meal had to be in their imagination. There was nothing there. Peter, it seemed, couldn't imagine a meal that good, so he was left with nothing. If Peter's reason prevailed, everyone would starve; if Peter could open up his imagination, he would join the rest of them in the celebration of abundance. The scene ends with an out-of-control food fight and a celebration so grand that even Peter could see it.

Part of Peter Pan's journey is realizing that somewhere along the way he lost his childlike imagination. Long before, he had traded it in for logic and sensibility. As we are all expected to, he had left childhood behind and become an adult. Somewhere along the way, he was convinced that maturity equaled an absence of imagination. To dream is a thing of children; to imagine, a luxury adults cannot indulge in.

For me, that scene was both inspiring and depressing—it was inspiring to imagine the endless possibilities if we could somehow materialize our dreams, and depressing because I became painfully aware that far too often good sense had replaced imagination in my own life. It is an interesting possibility, though, that there is a reality waiting to be materialized if we could trust in our dreams. Somehow, if we could only believe, we would be conduits bringing imagination into reality. And while perhaps we don't have the luxury of living in Neverland—where if we just believe hard enough, all the things we long for come into existence— there may be an underlying truth to this fable that we cannot afford to miss.

We artisans are created to transform the invisible into the visible. The creative act is a manifestation of imagination. Everything that exists began as an idea; everything we define as reality began as nothing more than imagination. Reality exists because it was first imagined. In fact, everything we know about the invisible comes to us in the form of the visible. Everything we know about God is translated through the things God created. God rested from his work of creating only when that creation was a complete manifestation of his imagination.

What was only an idea in the mind of God in verse 1 of Genesis 1 existed in totality by verse 31. Genesis 2:1 simply says, "Thus the heavens and the earth were completed in all their vast array." This is an elegant way of saying that the creative process was complete.

The author of Hebrews indicates that understanding the relationship between imagination and image is critical to understanding who God is and how he works. It is also essential to understanding how God works in and through us. Note that I am not saying that God stopped being creative at the end of the sixth day: everything God does is an act of creativity. This realization changes our understanding of who God is, as well as how God works in relationship to human beings.

Hebrews 11:1 reminds us, "Now faith is confidence in what we hope for and assurance about what we do not see. This is what the ancients were commended for." I have always been intrigued by the second half of that statement, but what is it that the ancients were commended for?

Hebrews 11:2 goes on to say, "By faith we understand that the universe was formed at God's command." That is a summary of Genesis 1. The next part of this verse is critical: "So that what is seen was not made out of what was visible."

The writer of Hebrews is reminding us of not only the creative process but also the material for the creative act. The ancients were commended for understanding that the physical world was created out of spiritual material—that what is seen was made not out of what was visible but out of what was invisible. The source material for the entire physical universe is the imagination of God. The ancients were commended for living in a unique relationship to this invisible reality. They were certain of what they did not see. Most of us struggle to be certain about what we do see.

God spoke the universe into existence with the material with which he started this creative endeavor, but that material was not made out of the visible. It shouldn't surprise us, then, that we who are created in the image of God are designed to engage life through the same process. We first dream; then we create. We first think; then we act. Even the Scriptures remind us that as a man thinks, so is he. Our internal world informs and forms our external world. Our inner lives provide the material from which we live out our lives. There is a universe inside us—a universe of thoughts, ideas, and dreams; a universe of fears, doubts, and questions; a universe of hopes, ambitions, and passions. Eventually the creative process demands that we choose from this invisible material, select what matters to us most, and materialize that imagination into reality.

You don't have to be Einstein to know that imagination is more powerful than knowledge, yet practical, everyday life seems to press us into an imaginationless reality. The longer we live, the more we become practical and reasonable. But if, at the core of what it means to be human, we are genuinely intended to be artisans, then imagination is never supplemental. It is always essential. The human imagination is perhaps the most distinct, unique, and valuable expression of being human. From a purely anthropological perspective, the ability to translate imagination into reality is a uniquely human attribute. Beavers build dams and bees build hives and ants build colonies, but humans are creatures not of simple instinct but of divine imagination. Humans create futures that exist only in the imagination. Every species builds, but humans create. Why in the world would we want to outgrow the influence and effect of the human imagination?

Several years ago, I was invited to a conversation at Columbia University in New York City. The subject was "What can be known?" On the panel were one of the university's premier scientists and the head of the Department of Humanities, who was a Kantian philosopher. After the opening remarks, I knew for certain that I should have come better prepared. In an auditorium filled with hundreds of students and faculty, it was not difficult to ascertain that my faith put me in a slim minority.

The scientist explained that only what can be proven empirically can be known. The professor of humanities, informed by the teachings of Kant, stated that what can be known is human action and therefore ethics. For a person who believes that what is seen was not made out of the visible, this is a particularly uncomfortable space to stand in, in a room filled with people who are convinced that all that exists is what can be seen.

So I admitted up front, "I cheated. I know things I

shouldn't know. I know I'm not empirically supposed to know God or know things that exist in the invisible, but I'm reminded of the conversation between Peter and Jesus where Jesus asks Peter, 'Who do you say that I am?' And Peter says, 'You're the Christ, the son of the living God.' Then Jesus says to Peter, essentially, 'You cheated. You got the right answer, but it wasn't because you studied.' He said specifically, 'Flesh and blood have not revealed this to you, but my Father who is in heaven.'

"The curious thing about knowing is that there are an endless number of layers of knowing. We can know two plus two is four; we can know that pi is an endless series of numbers that go off into infinity without even understanding what infinity is; we can know that the universe is ever expanding, although we have no experience of it; we can know there is dark matter and dark energy because of everything we don't know; we can know that we are in love but don't know why or how. We humans are highly complex knowing machines. There are so many different layers to knowing. So we shouldn't rule out the possibility that it's within our human capacity to also know God."

After a wonderful conversation with two of the most interesting people I have had the opportunity to dialogue with in a long time, we moved to the Q&A. From my perspective, an endless number of questions on three-by-five cards were turned in. When I watched them divide the cards, there was a question or two for the scientist and a question or two for the philosopher and a stack of questions clearly coming my way. One of those questions stood out, though, and has never left me: "When you were a child, you had imaginary friends like Santa Claus and the Tooth Fairy and God. Why did you get rid of your other imaginary friends and keep God?"

Even now, I still love this question. With very little time to construct a thoughtful response, I approached it like this: "First of all, it's clear you don't know me if you think I've given up my imaginary friends. Yes, you're right that when I was a small child I had imaginary friends like Santa Claus, the Tooth Fairy, the giant rabbit that hid in my closet and only came out at night (but that's a different story), and God. I suppose if you conclude that all your imaginary friends are constructs of your imagination, then eventually all those imaginary friends should disappear with maturity. When my son, Aaron, was a little boy, he wouldn't eat his vegetables, but strangely enough he would go in the backyard and eat rocks. More than once we had to chase Aaron down and dig into his mouth and pull out the dirt and rocks that he was so determined to swallow and digest. But he wouldn't eat his mother's cooking, which was no small discouragement to Kim. No matter how hard she tried or how many different ways she threatened him, he would just look at those vegetables, and neither heaven nor earth could make him open his mouth and even give them a try.

"So one day I said to Kim, 'I have an idea. Let's just take the vegetables, throw them in the backyard, and put him outside to play. Maybe he'll start eating them with the dirt and the rocks.'

"My wife, Kim, didn't think this was the guide to better parenting, so the strategy was a no-go. But we didn't give up on Aaron. We kept feeding him vegetables and working to convince him that rocks are bad for his teeth and terrible for the digestion. Eventually he got it. I can tell you with great certainty and no small amount of pride that my twenty-four-year-old son no longer eats dirt and rocks and loves every variety of fruits and vegetables. Fortunately for Aaron, just because he couldn't distinguish between peas and rocks, we didn't give up on proper meals. In the same way, just because when you are a kid you can't distinguish between Santa Claus and God, you don't give up on your imagination and assume that all your imaginary friends need to be extricated from your life. You see, if your imaginary friend somehow transforms your life, makes you a better human being, moves you from arrogance to humility, from greed to generosity, from hate to love—if this imaginary friend changes everything for you and makes you the kind of human being you've always longed to be but could never find the strength to become alone—do not, I repeat *do not,* ever give up on that imaginary friend, because that imaginary friend who changes everything for the good is the most real thing you'll ever know."

Is it possible that the human imagination is the playground of God, that while we fill the imagination with Santa Claus and the Tooth Fairy and the Easter Bunny, our imagination was always intended to be the place where humans could interact with God? Only in our imagination can we begin to contain even the smallest expression of the bigness of God; only in our imagination can we accomplish anything, go anywhere, or become anyone; only in our imagination do we have boundless possibilities and endless potential; only in our imagination can we even begin to conceive of what reality might become if it began to reflect the imagination of God. In our imagination, conversations that come from someone who is all-knowing and all-powerful and all-present, for whom all things are possible, can be engaged at a human level.

The reason I didn't give up on God when I put away my other imaginary friends is that every time I create more room by vacating an imaginary friend, I find more space for those extraordinary encounters with the living God.

One of the great challenges in my early journey of faith was the seemingly perpetual war between creativity and spirituality. The faith journey seemed a product more of education and information than of imagination and passion. To be perfectly frank, I have never met God by studying a doctrine, but I have met God over and over listening to my dreams. The life of faith is less about gathering information than it is about expanding imagination. The movement Jesus started was a movement of dreamers and visionaries, not a movement of academics and theologians. The soul feeds on the imagination; the artist lives in the imagination. Imagination always precedes creativity. To engage in the creative act, you must be comfortable working with invisible material. Then comes the tricky part—materializing that invisible material. It's about moving imagination into image, transforming the invisible into the visible.

Have you ever noticed that you're more awesome in your imagination than you are in real life? I have often felt stunted by reality's effect on my talent. In my imagination, I can sing. I am the male version of Adele. If you could hear what I can hear, it would blow you away. But when I take that same extraordinary talent and try to exercise it in the real world, somehow my talent diminishes. In fact, if I were to be specific, if I could pin this down to the exact moment when my extraordinary talent becomes painfully ordinary, it's that moment when somebody else hears me sing. I am so clearly great in my imagination, but people keep letting me down. Reality keeps hurting my chances of having an extraordinary musical career. I can't seem to translate the experience in my imagination into the experience that plays out in reality.

My daughter, Mariah, on the other hand, seems to be able to translate what she hears in her head to what we hear when she sings. When we hear her sing, it's like stepping into a dream. That may be one way we discover our unique artistic space—that point where reality matches imagination. This may be the best indicator of a natural talent or where we find our natural sweet spot: how closely does our execution resemble our imagination? Part of the uniqueness of being human is that we are materializers of the invisible. We discover what we do best in life when we see something in our imagination and are then able to execute it in the real world. Sometimes this process works in reverse. I tried to water-ski once and failed miserably. Then I spent the summer working at SeaWorld, watching world-class skiers while trapped selling Cokes inside a kiosk. Without realizing it, I spent the summer watching, observing, and imagining myself performing the same feats that those skilled entertainers had spent a lifetime developing.

To my surprise, the next time I skied, I could slalom effortlessly. I had been practicing in my imagination all summer long, and given the opportunity, I was able to translate it into reality.

Have you ever had an idea of yourself that was different from what played out in real life? More often than not, our focus is talent—to become a great doctor, a great teacher, a great writer, a great attorney. And it's completely human to imagine ourselves as the very best in a field for which we have a deep passion. How many of us haven't imagined ourselves as the next LeBron James or the next Tiger Woods or the next Steven Spielberg or the next Maya Angelou? I am reminded of the endless people I have met who quickly described themselves as an "idea person." Why is it that more often than not the person who says "I am an idea guy" usually means "I don't actually like doing work" or "I have no specific skill set" or "I can tell you what to do, but someone else will have to figure out how to do it." The only ideas that really matter are the ones that get turned into realities. There is no proof of creativity without action. The creative act requires both sides: it requires creativity, and it requires action.

For years, I signed all my books with three simple words—dream, risk, create. Each reminds me of the reason most of us never go from dreaming to creating: it's an uncomfortable middle space called risk.

If the culminating moment of God's creative act was the creation of man, then it is clear that we cannot create without risk. God's ultimate act of creation— creating humanity in his own likeness, with the freedom to choose so that we might become authentic conduits of love—was the greatest risk that God ever undertook.

I love God's words to Jeremiah (1:5), when he reminds him, "Before I formed you in the womb I knew you, before you were born I set you apart; I appointed you as a prophet to the nations."

This is the intimate application of everything we have been talking about applied here to a specific individual. What God is saying to Jeremiah also goes for us: "I knew you before you were born." How is it possible to know someone before he was born, unless for God the relationship begins while we are only an idea in his mind. Jeremiah, you were a dream in the heart of God, an idea in the mind of God, a manifestation of imagination. You exist because God uses invisible material to make all things visible.

Somehow it is exhilarating to me to realize that I was an idea in the mind of God before I was an embryo in the womb of my mother. Everyone knows that the quality of a product is directly related to the material used, the process chosen, and the artist who designs and creates it. For us, all of those are rooted in God. We were formed in the mind of God, designed by the hand of God, and created in the image of God. The fingerprints of God are all over us. But this is only how the process began.

Like a master artist, God entrusts us with the critical phase in the process we call life. This leads to the most important question: What is your idea of you? Who is it that you have decided to become? If your greatest work of art is the life you live, and ultimately life is a creative act, what life will you choose to leave behind as your masterpiece?

Who we were created to become already exists in the mind of God. It's placed in our physical DNA and in the longings of our soul. Our lives are supposed to be a manifestation of the imagination of God, and whatever else we leave behind—the life we choose to live and the person we choose to become—is the ultimate expression of the artisan soul.

What is inescapable is that we have been designed by God as a creative being. Each day that we walk this earth, whether we recognize it or not, we are in the process of creating. Our work, like God's, is to create. One question remains: What are we creating? What are we leaving in the wake of our lives? The words we speak, the choices we make, the actions we take are the material from which we not only create our lives but create the world around us.

Some have chosen to take this creative gift and turn it into a destructive force. That's an inherent risk when you design a creature as a creative being. Have you ever met someone who was unbelievably creative in causing pain and wreaking havoc on the world around them? If we choose as our tools violence, greed, bitterness, and vengeance, our creative gifts will bring pain and devastation to the world around us. But if we understand our lives as the canvas God has entrusted us to create, if we realize that our lives are to reflect the nature and essence of God, then we will choose to expand those things that reflect the heart and character of God. When we choose to create as an act of love, we join forces with the Creator of the universe and become givers of life.

Here we must move from being more than simply artists, to being designers as well. The artisan soul is driven by more than simple reflecting; it is driven by creating. Though far too often art is nothing more than a catharsis bringing relief to the deepest longings of our souls, the nature of our design demands of us far more responsibility than to create art for art's sake. The truth of the matter is that all art has an underlying narrative for which it advocates; all art is a declaration of meaning or the lack of it; all art is created both for self-expression and for the extension of self. Art changes the world, which is why art cannot be left in the hands of an elite few. We must embrace the critical realities that everyone is an artist, that everyone creates, and that everyone is responsible for the creative act. So if we are created by God and created by God to create, then the divine process must inform our process.

Long before design thinking became popular in the modern landscape of organizational and behavioral science, it was the blueprint of the opening chapter of the Scriptures. If a critical attribute of design thinking is to begin with the end in mind, from that end moving through synthesis to create the most human and organic process, then we find the pinnacle of that expression in Genesis 1. The Hebraic language reminds us that repetition exists for emphasis. You know what matters because they make sure you can't miss it.

The recurring phrases in Genesis 1 are built around two significant words—*good* and *living.* Everything God created was good, and that speaks of the essence of the creative act. The purpose of that creative act, though, is centered in that second word—everything was created for life. The sweeping movements of the creation of the universe, the creation of the sun and moon, the creation of the solar system, the creation of earth, the creation of the waters and the land— everything was created with the intention of creating a sustaining life. After the creation of the physical universe on this planet, the earth becomes the ultimate sustainer of life. It creates living beings—living beings that walk the earth, living beings that fly in the air, and living beings that swim in the oceans. The driving narrative of the story of creation is that the entire universe was designed with one particular outcome: living beings. And if the driving intention of the universe was life, then God's preeminent creative act happened on the sixth day, when he created man as a living being.

So if we apply design thinking backward, beginning with the end in mind, the ultimate end of the creative process was God's intention to create a living being designed in his image. Everything was created to sustain life for us. We may disagree with the summary of the existence of the universe, but the Scriptures begin with the basic declaration that the entire cosmos was created so that you and I could live. We find all the essential ingredients for design thinking in this creative process. For design to exist, there has to be intention, and everything in the opening narrative of the Scriptures is permeated with the intention of God.

The narrative of creation has for far too long been the center point of a battle between science and mythology, and all the while we keep missing the point. The point of Genesis is that God created us with intention, that the entire universe exists with intention, and that we, if we are to live life as God intended, must also live intentional lives. Ironically, everything else in creation lives within its intention without choice. Apple trees create apples—no debate. Happens every time. Antelopes give birth to antelopes; flounder spawn flounder. This creation is designed to be part of the creative process. Everything creates of its own kind. This, too, is a reoccurring phrase in Genesis 1.

Everything is created with intention. Nothing is arbitrary or meaningless. Humanity is God's culminating act of creativity, designed with the highest intention to reflect most personally the likeness of God. Ironically, we who were created with the highest intention were also created with the capacity to deny, betray, or demean that intention. Whereas a horse will always live as a horse is intended to live, humans may live inhumane lives.

The artisan soul reclaims its intention. We understand that with creative freedom comes creative responsibility. When we live our lives without intention, it is like throwing paint against the wall and pretending that it's art—unless, of course, when we are throwing that paint against the wall, there is intentionality behind it. If God's intention was to ensure the re-creation of life, we should choose no lesser intention for our lives. Every word, every action, every creative act should have as its ultimate intention to bring life to others.

Remember, intention precedes creation, and essence informs intention. We cannot create life if we are not alive. Which for me brings new meaning and clarity to the words of Jesus, "I have come that they may have life, and have it to the full" (John 10:10). Not only is the creative process driven by intention, but it is also driven by relationship. Nothing in the creative process was designed in isolation. Creation was designed as an organic whole.

While a cursory glance at part of the creative process might lead someone to assume that one aspect of creation has nothing to do with the other, science itself has proved to us that quite the opposite is true. Regardless of what we discover, regardless of how far we are able to explore or how profound our discoveries may be, every nuance of the universe, every detail of the creative order, only magnifies the extraordinary integration of all things. Simply put, the unifying principle of the universe is relationship.

Thousands of years ago, before science began to inform the human narrative, the writer of Genesis understood that God didn't simply throw the sun up into the sky. Long before we understood the critical nature of design, the Hebrews understood that the universe was designed with a relational intelligence that could not possibly be accidental. It's no small thing that the universe somehow got it all right, that the distance between the sun and the earth just happened to be exactly right, and the atmosphere just happened to be exactly what the human species needed to survive. It didn't just happen that in the midst of a planet with salt water, the freshwater essential to our survival erupted out of the earth. What if there had only been salt water? What if nitrogen filled the atmosphere?

However you understand humanity's relationship to nature, we are intimately connected to the entire created order. Just as plants depend on us, we depend on them. What we inhale, they exhale. What we exhale, they inhale. We live in symbiosis. We live in relationship with all things. It shouldn't surprise us, when we are created for relationship with each other and in relationship to the created order, that we are also created for relationship with the Creator of the universe.

In the paradise known as Eden, we are told, God saw that it was not good for man to be alone. We are relational creatures living in a universe held together by relationship. There may be no more powerful or elegant example of design through synthesis than the one we find in the opening pages of the Scriptures. A unique characteristic of design thinking is that the process is informed less by the product than by the people it serves. All design is in a sense informed by ergonomics. What matters is how what we create affects and serves humanity. This characteristic of the design process can be described as empathy, which means we begin the entire process by asking a question: How does this affect others?

The highest level of design is a deep commitment to reclaiming our humanity. I love how the creative act in Genesis 1 begins with the almost ethereal creation of light out of darkness and ends with an intimate act of God breathing life into man. This is the best reflection and highest expression of design thinking. Everything drives toward intimacy. The culminating moment of the creative act is the moment when man awakens and finds his meaning in God. The greater the design, the more intimate its expression. From beginning to end, the Scriptures are clear that though the unifying principle of the universe is relationship and its driving force is intention, the motivation for the creation of all things is love.

Within the universe's intention and its unique design around relationship, we find that the focal point of the universe, the motive of the universe, is love. God created life so that we could know love. Everything God does is an expression of his love. It is neither trite nor superficial that the Scriptures summarize this in three simple words: "God is love." It is critical to understand this because, if we are to reclaim our role in the creative process and express our lives as masterful works of art, we, too, must be sure that our motivation is the expansion of love. Jesus made this the central proof of living in relationship with him. "A new command I give you: Love one another. As I have loved you, so you must love one another. By this everyone will know that you are my disciples, if you love one another" (John 13:34–35).

If we have embraced God's intention and stepped into relationship with God, then we, too, will live out our lives with God's motive. When love is the driving force of the universe, everything moves toward intimacy; everything is informed by empathy; everything we create brings life.

Nearly five years ago, I made a career shift and found myself in the world of fashion. I quickly learned that all design is informed by story and that in the end fashion is all about storytelling.

The story that shapes who we are informs everything we make, and it works on multiple levels. Brands tell us a story to inspire us to participate. If we buy a pair of shoes, we will be better athletes; if we buy a certain jacket, we will become more adventurous; if we wear a certain perfume, we will be more glamorous. Even social innovation has entered the world of fashion, understanding that we can tell a great story by selling a pair of shoes. What we wear is an extension of who we are, or at least of who we want to be perceived to be.

One of the curious experiences I had during those years in the fashion industry was that any encounter with an old-school craftsman, whether from Europe or the Middle East, always began with a long conversation. They would tell their story of how they moved into leatherwork or working with fabrics, or whatever their particular arena in the process was. Then they would ask me my story. They wanted to understand my intention. They needed to decide if they wanted to have a relationship with us. It was never simply about making a product; the product was always for them an extension of themselves.

Every time I met with one of the owners of the various manufacturing companies we interacted with, they always said to me, "You are far more European than American." I heard this over and over. At first I would simply nod and take it as a compliment, although admittedly I had no idea what they meant. I'm an immigrant, so I thought they were picking up on that, and I'm proud to be an American, so I wasn't sure what the nuanced distinction was. But when I heard it again on a particular trip, I paused and asked, "What exactly does it mean that I am more European than American?"

The elderly salesman very quickly and easily explained, "American fashion is about figuring out how to sell a product, and a story is contrived so that the product will sell. European fashion is always about a lifestyle and is always built on the authentic life lived out by the individual who inspires the brand.

The fashion then becomes an extension of that person's values and lifestyle. A European does not try to create for the purpose of selling; he knows that his unique style will find its own audience when it finds the person who resonates with the story."

As an immigrant to the United States, I have so much respect and appreciation for what it means to be an American, but I must confess that there are some European values I admire over American ones. When I have had the privilege of traveling across Europe, I have seen the beauty that comes when a person lives a life reflective of the authentic self. Of course, I have seen this many times here, as I traveled across the states, but I do think that we are far more susceptible to losing ourselves in the attempt to be what others want us to be rather than rooting ourselves in the person we were created to be. Though market research invests a lot of money in deciding who we are, living our lives based on the opinions of others will only cause us to lose our souls and our way.

It was no small challenge working through the process of learning to translate the things we cared about into an everyday commodity. How do we express our values and essence in a medicine bag? How can we pass on our story in the design of a men's suit? If my journey into this industry has taught me anything, it is that not only is it possible, but it is essential.

It is essential not only in fashion but in every arena of human engagement. Our best lives are lived out when we are driven by our deepest passions in the task of turning our dreams into reality. Once we know what our story is, it becomes easier and easier to know how to write the next chapter.

Years ago, when I moved to Los Angeles, I met a young woman named Kristin Ross. She worked for the president of a film company and seemed destined for a promising career in the industry. It was another classic story of a mid-America kid from Michigan coming to Los Angeles to pursue a dream of Holly-wood success. All who came to know her were certain that she was a shoo-in for a successful career as a director. But, like so many people in Los Angeles, her talent, intelligence, and hard work did not result in the materialization of her dream. Kristin is proof that you can give everything to a dream and still not have it materialize. In her own words, she became bitter and disillusioned.

During this journey, she met a man named Chad Lauterbach, and eventually this woman who was married to her career decided it would be better to be married to Chad. This in no way diminished her ambition or determination. Soon she came to the realization that her film career was not going to happen, and her marriage suffered as she struggled through the death of a dream. To add to the challenge, she unexpectedly became pregnant, and though she had never imagined herself as a mom, she gave birth to a beautiful little girl.

One of the quirky things about Kristin is that she is a purist about everything. She describes herself as "a bit neurotic and somewhat crazy." When it comes to organic versus artificial anything, neurotic would be an understatement. She reads every label, laments all the artificiality in the world, knows every chemical is out to get her, and to the best of her ability has built a world of only natural and organic products for herself and her family. She is highly sensitive to processed foods, and her skin is, as she would put it, "supersensitive" to anything unnatural or artificial. So, of course, she started making her own lotions, soaps, and bath products. She even went as far as making her own natural deodorant. One day she brought me a package of gifts—shampoos, soaps, and deodorants that you could most likely eat. In fact, I discovered they *were* mostly edible. She started a homegrown company called Root Beauty. In her own words, "Root Beauty is an all-natural, organic skin care line with ingredients that you can not only pronounce but are mostly edible." I guess in some ways it solves both of her problems—her delicate relationship to both food and skin care products.

What I love about Kristin's story is that she didn't sit around asking herself, "How can I make myself rich and successful?" After the death of her dream of becoming a filmmaker, finding herself in a state of angst as a wife and mother, she began to apply the same talents that had brought her to the end of a dream to creating something that would meet a real need in her own life, as well as serving the people she cared about the most. Kristin's struggle to find beauty products that were both natural and effective led her to experiment with and create products of her own at home for herself and her friends.

Kristin imagined a world in which severe sensitivities to the chemicals we are confronted with every day could be eliminated, and she translated that idea into a reality through creativity, determination, and hard work. She took her story, and by paying careful attention to a real need that was right in front of her, she began to express her most creative self while making the world a better place.

Years ago someone said to me, "Erwin, you either define yourself or let yourself be defined by others." And the adage is true: *define or be defined.* We either let ourselves become products of the intention of others or products of living an intentional life. We are creatures designed for relationship, and either we are shaped by the relationships that choose us or we choose our relationships on the basis of the person we intend to become.

Every artist must have a motivation; every creative act is the materialization of the invisible. Everything we do is a manifestation of imagination. Since part of our creative responsibility is to move from imagination to image, we need to take every thought captive to the obedience of Christ and allow our imagination once again to be the playground of God. And once our dreams and visions are the material that has been passed on to us by a divine imagination, then it is time to dream, to risk, and to create.

Craft

The Elegance of Workmanship

Mozart found his genius at an early age. His full name was Johannes Chrysostomus Wolfgangus Theophilus Mozart, but because of his profound talent, he is known to the world simply as Mozart. There may be no name more famous among composers than Mozart. By the age of five, he was already composing and performing at a level that most of us could only aspire to in a lifetime. By seventeen, he was serving as the court musician in Salzburg. By his early twenties, he was refining the greatest pieces the world would ever know. Some people find "it" early, and what they find is a treasure to the world. It is hard to imagine that Mozart composed over six hundred works, most of which would be considered masterpieces by the time he was thirty-five. Then again, he didn't live to see his thirty-sixth birthday.

More often than not, when we think of talent or genius, we envisage people who are both prodigies and prodigious. This is even truer today. In competitive cosmopolitan areas, we find parents putting their children in pre-pre-pre-schools by the age of two. In fact, there are some places where you can ensure your child has a distinct advantage by starting training at six months. Partly, this reflects parents' deep commitment to giving their child the best chance for success. Partly, it is parents' ever-present hope of releasing a child's inner Mozart.

If our parents were unsuccessful in unleashing the genius within us, we may find ourselves spending the rest of our lives in search of our inner Bobby Fischer. He was perhaps the greatest chess master ever. At thirteen, he won what became known as the game of the century. Starting at fourteen, he played in eight U.S. championships, winning each by at least a point. At fifteen and a half, he became the youngest grand master in the world. Before he could drive or legally buy alcohol, he had achieved the only perfect score in the history of the U.S. championship.

Like Mozart, Bobby Fischer accomplished his greatest feats before the age of thirty-five. Everything after that point was downhill. Though the lives of these individuals are inspiring, if not overwhelming, they reinforce a mythology of greatness that produces a false idea of how greatness is achieved. This mythology of greatness is reinforced by the popular heroes of our time. Whether we look to icons like Michael Jordan and Tiger Woods or celebrate the extraordinary achievements by the likes of Michael Phelps and Gabby Douglas, the idea that greatness comes at an early age or not at all is reinforced in our cultural psyche. The fact that Michael Phelps broke a world record in the two-hundred-meter butterfly at the age of fifteen years and nine months, then retired as the greatest Olympian of all time at twenty-seven only makes it more painful for us underachievers. It is inspiring and debilitating at the same time. Gabby Douglas became the first African-American to ever win Olympic gold in women's gymnastics. She became the best in the world at sixteen.

At sixteen, I wasn't the best in the world at anything. By twenty-seven, I was clearly not gold-medal material. If I had embraced their lives and their stories as the story of all of us, I would have jumped off a bridge at twenty-nine. After all, what's the point? We get one shot to be great, and then we turn twenty-one. We have one opportunity to do something meaningful with our lives, and if that doesn't happen, we are condemned to a life of mundane adulthood. Maybe that's why the drinking age is twenty-one; we have to find solace for our undeniable ineptness somewhere.

Is it possible that the reason these individuals provide such inspiration is that they are exceptions to the rule? We live in a world where the value of human lives has been flipped upside down. In ancient times, it was understood that the young were at the start of their journeys and that those who had lived long, colorful lives were sources of wisdom and insight. The greatest contributors to the world were the ones who had lived longest and best. The young admired the old; the novice treasured the opportunity to travel with those who had so much to teach.

Modern culture has flipped that upside down. The most popular arenas where talent is displayed to the popular audience are those fields where youth is the greatest advantage. I recently heard someone explain in an interview that it isn't difficult to figure out when an athlete is using performance-enhancing drugs. His reasoning was simple: When you are forty years old and competing at a world-class level against twenty-five-year-olds, you're using drugs. It is inescapable that there are arenas in life where the young have the greatest advantage, whether it is in professional sports or popular music or a particular discipline where the talent of our youth is exactly the talent that is needed. But to believe this is how our lives are supposed to work is a terrible misunderstanding of how greatness emerges and develops.

It is one thing to find a unique talent upon which to build a life; it's another thing to build a life as a work of art. That process takes a lifetime. I always hoped some unique talent would emerge from my life at an early age, but that never happened. In fact, after five decades, I have come to realize that for most of us the discovery and development of our talents is less like finding gold sitting on the surface and more like spending a lifetime drilling deep into the earth in search of undiscovered oil. It takes a lifetime for most of us to bring our talents to the surface and turn them into the material from which we build our lives. The most hopeful description in my youth was that I was a jack-of-all-trades and the master of none. The painful realization happened when I came face-to-face with the truth. I wasn't even a jack-of-all-trades; it was only an assumption made because I was the master of none.

It seems like I have had a thousand different jobs over the last five decades. I mowed lawns, bussed tables, became a waiter, became a chef—no, that's an overstatement: became a cook—was a lumberjack, worked as a carpenter, worked construction, put insulation into attics, picked oranges in the orange groves, worked as a painter and as a librarian, did

landscaping, worked as a counselor, became a basketball referee and a football referee, all the while starting churches and social service organizations among
the poor, which is very similar to being unemployed.
I also worked as a metropolitan consultant, an urban-
ologist, a futurist, a professional speaker and a distin-
guished lecturer for a couple of universities, designed
master's and doctoral programs for universities, and
became the creative director of my own fashion company. Today I find myself working as an artist and
as a writer and as a director, as a producer and as an
entrepreneur. So let me summarize: I have had years
of unemployment, moving from one thing to another,
always trying to find that arena where I could best
express the person God has made me and express
the talents that I still have to believe he has placed
within me. Thirty years ago I could have never imagined that I would one day have the privilege of creating a place like Mosaic and still have the opportunity
to work as a writer, filmmaker, and artist.

I envy those people who early on identified a singular talent, knew exactly what they were born to do,
and spent their entire lives doing it well. They have
a distinct advantage over people like me. They just
keep getting better and better and better at what they
already did better than everyone else. But here's the
unifying theme between those who find their unique
talent at an early age and those for whom that talent

takes a lifetime to develop: greatness never emerges outside of hard work.

We sometimes forget that the seventeen-year-old world champion decided early on to vacate childhood and take the attitude of a professional. By the age of sixteen, Gabby Douglas had already put in the ten thousand hours of deliberate practice that is so often described as the essential ingredient for talent to find its highest expression. Mozart did nothing but compose; Fischer lived, ate, and breathed chess; Jordan's entire world revolved around basketball. I am convinced that regardless of how extraordinary their raw talent was in childhood, that potential would have never become the brilliant expression of human genius without hard work. Eventually art becomes craft. The combination of talent and passion funneled through the crucible of discipline and determination resulted in an expression of skill and execution that was later deemed greatness and genius.

The times I have had the opportunity to be on a film or TV set, I have always been amazed at the creative energy that fills the atmosphere and the extraordinary commitment to excellence that each production demands. It's exhilarating to stand behind a camera and watch actors of extraordinary talent lay out a scene. It's inspiring to watch a great director as he orchestrates people and technology to create a moment that moves us deeply. If you have the opportunity to interact with cast and crew, you quickly realize that talent layers through every aspect of the filmmaking process.

I remember in one of the first projects I had the opportunity to direct, I was working through how to best use lighting in a scene where it was raining outside a Macy's parking lot. I walked over to an older man working the crane, which was our primary lighting source for this shot. I casually began to interview him about his life and work. He explained to me that he had been working on films for over twenty years. I quickly discovered that he had worked with some of the world's best directors, so I began to inquire in as casual a tone as I could, "So if, let's say, Spielberg was shooting this scene, how would he do this lighting? Or if it was Scorsese?"

I began drawing on his wealth of experience and realized that even though I was the director, in reality I was the student and he was the teacher. From lighting to sound, every grip and technician has a wealth of knowledge and experience, and more often than not, all that expertise is left untapped by those who do not realize they can learn from everyone. My volunteer cinematographer had been the secondary cinematographer for Terrence Malick's film *The Thin Red Line*. I guarantee you that most of our conversations consisted of me asking questions and then listening carefully while he answered. I quickly learned that the best way to produce your best work is to surround yourself with people who are committed to always bringing their best work.

Still, of all the moments I have had behind the camera, shooting from helicopters and directing underwater scenes, nothing matches what you experience at craft services—what the rest of the world knows as catering. I learned quickly that the better the set, crew, and cast, the better the food. I don't know if I have ever had better food in my life, or in greater abundance and variety, than when I sneaked in line to experience the artistry of the men and women who serve in craft services. At first I was surprised, but later it made perfect sense. If you expect the best lighting, the best sound, the best set design, the best performances, and the best directing, then you should of course provide the best food.

The same philosophy can be found in professional sports. When I had the opportunity to visit with the Green Bay Packers, I was given a tour of their extraordinary operation. Every detail mattered, from the quotes on the walls to the photographs and trophies hung in the halls for inspiration, from the expertise in the training room to the world-class execution in their kitchen. It would not be an exaggeration to say that the center of that universe was the area in which the team ate meals—with multiple options carefully orchestrated to fuel the optimal performance of every athlete on the team.

What I learned behind the scenes on a movie set and in professional sports is that there is a critical process that demands our highest engagement and execution if we are to achieve optimal performance. For some reason, somewhere along the way, the spectrum of creativity pushed the idea of art and craft in opposite directions.

Years ago in our community at Mosaic, we began designating the different tribes that served together. *Developers* worked in child development; *connectors* helped guests make friends and find a place to belong; *artisans* focused on the performing arts; and *craftsmen* created the infrastructure that allowed us to perform at the highest level of execution. I found it interesting that those designations were readily received by the groups, except for the craftsmen. *Craftsman* was perceived as a demeaning, even derogatory, designation. Yet the reality is that all of us are craftsmen. If we are going to live out the highest expression of who we are, we must recognize that the true artisan is also a true craftsman.

The artisan soul embraces and celebrates the elegance of workmanship. We understand that something becomes a work of art only because there is an artist at work—that, in fact, art plus work equals craft. The craftsman is the individual who goes beyond inspiration. This is where a lot of us get tripped up. We have come to believe that if we have a natural talent, creativity should come easily, especially when we add God to the mix. If God has given us this talent, if our talent is a gift from God himself, then shouldn't it just come naturally? Shouldn't the expression and development of that talent come easily? I think there is a subtle misunderstanding when it comes to gifts and talents and how they play out in real life.

We hope that discovering our talents, and even our calling or purpose, will lead us to effortless success. I would propose that the exact opposite is true: if God created us to be successful at something, then he has called us to work hard at it. I am absolutely convinced that a spiritual gift and hard work were never intended to be mutually exclusive. Potential is talent that has not been harnessed; it is what talent looks like when it is undisciplined. Potential is how we describe your extraordinary nature before you have gained mastery over that potential.

Talent, when fully developed, becomes a strength. When we have mastery over our talent, we gain almost superhuman strength. For me, it is illuminating that the etymology of *craft* goes back to an Old High German word meaning "strength." The word *strength* later took on the additional meaning of "skill," and from the concept of skill formed out of strength comes artistry. Every creative endeavor that a human being masters becomes a craft. Every creative endeavor involves the integration of passion and discipline, the intersection of talent and skill. Every creative endeavor is both compulsion and determination. Anything we aspire to do as an expression of our artisan soul requires inspiration and strength. And while inspiration has been overvalued, the importance of strength has been understated.

It is not incidental that when David calls Solomon to build the temple, he says to his son, "Be strong and courageous, and do the work. Do not be afraid or discouraged, for the Lord God, my God, is with you. He will not fail you or forsake you until all the work for the service of the temple of the Lord is finished. The divisions of the priests and Levites are ready for all the work on the temple of God, and every willing person skilled in any craft will help you in all the work. The officials and all the people will obey your every command" (1 Chronicles 28:20–21).

David's admonition to Solomon is not "be inspired and creative" but "be strong and courageous." Certainly the building of the temple was one of the most inspired and creative endeavors known to man. History proves that Solomon was never lacking in genius or ingenuity. Here, though, we find the secret to his success and perhaps the secret to ours: to do our greatest work, we must overcome the temptation to be afraid or become discouraged, engaging the creative process with strength and courage.

Isn't this a strange time for exhorting someone to be strong and courageous? I can understand language like that when talking to Joshua, about to go to war as he enters the Promised Land. It makes perfect sense to remind a shepherd boy about to face a giant that he should be strong and courageous. If someone is about to be thrown into a lions' den, I understand why the pep talk would be, "Remember, be strong and courageous." But Solomon is facing none of that. He lived in a time of peace and prosperity, yet the work that God created him to do would require the same mettle that David found inside himself when picking up five smooth stones. I want to assure you that if you are determined to live the life that God created you to live, if you are committed to making your life your most creative act, if you resolve to do nothing less than to make your life your greatest work of art, you will need the same strength and courage that David hoped for his son Solomon.

The Scriptures see work as a sacred space, and every sacred act requires both courage and strength. It is also important to note David's vision of how this immense project would be accomplished. It was a mission bigger than Solomon, so he reminds him that "every willing person skilled in any craft will help you in all the work."

Solomon was to bring together only the willing and only those who were skilled. I imagine there were many people who were willing but not skilled and others who were skilled but unwilling. Before taking on this great endeavor, he was first to bring together the right people to accomplish such a great task: Find the people who have a passion for their work and who have paid the price of honing their skills of their particular craft. Those are the people we want to bring together. Those are the people we want to build our future on.

You can be an architect, but to be the architect God created you to be requires strength and courage. You can be a teacher or an attorney or a financial planner, but to be the teacher or attorney or financial planner that God created you to be is going to require strength and courage. You can be a writer or a dancer or a painter, but to be the writer or dancer or painter that God created you to be is going to require strength and courage. Because if talent requires discipline to reach its highest expression, all the more does becoming the person God created you to be.

Like talent, character is formed through discipline. In my last book, *Wide Awake,* I laid out a process for all of us who know that we have much yet to accomplish. It's been a wonderful realization after fifty years of life that if we work hard enough, hard work will eventually be mistaken for talent. And if we refuse to give up, perseverance will eventually be mistaken for greatness.

Two of the most inspiring and talented craftsmen I have the privilege of knowing are Emerson

Nowotny and Christian Navarro. Emerson is a craftsman who chooses wood and stone as mediums for
his art form, as he creates environments that both
inspire people and bring them together. Emerson,
who is from Bolivia, started building with his father
when he was a small boy. At fifteen, he began working with a construction contractor to pay for rent. He
learned various trades and soon became a foreman
for the company. At twenty-six, he opened his first
restaurant and did the build-out himself; that's when
he began integrating construction and ambiance as
his context for art. Soon he owned two restaurants,
building them both himself. He now has been creating human spaces for eighteen years.

I love sitting down with Emerson, imagining what
a space could look like and feel like, and watching
him translate our imagination into reality. Everything Emerson touches is filled with warmth and
love. Every environment that he moves from design
into execution creates a sense of community while
making people feel as if they are walking through
an installation at a gallery. But don't kid yourself—
this never comes easily. I don't know anyone who
works longer hours or does harder work than Emerson. We benefit not only from his immense creativity but from his incomparable hard work. This is
what makes Emerson a craftsman.

Christian has chosen a different medium: he is

a gourmet chef. I have found numerous excuses to invite Christian to cater events here in Los Angeles. Everything he creates is visually stimulating as well as mouthwatering. Part of his presentation is to explain with each course how what we are about to experience reflects the way his food integrates his experiences as well as his expertise. Everything is a fusion of the different worlds through which Christian has passed. And whether it's an unusual integration of Mexican and Korean dishes or some unexpected meeting of Italian and Japanese, every course that Christian serves is an extension of his life and an expression of his story.

Christian began cooking professionally at twenty-two, though he began to experiment in the kitchen when he was ten. Fried rice, flan, and spaghetti bolognese are the first things he remembers making. He made his first meringue at twelve, when most of us were only eating it! He estimates that he has spent more than 22,000 hours cooking and has invested at least 17,000 hours working on his craft for the purpose of gaining mastery over the culinary arts.

His food is not only an extension of his past; it's also deeply rooted in the present. He uses only fresh and organic materials, cooking from what is available today. Thus the fish and spices and vegetables will change based on the best reflection of today's offering. At the same time, everything Christian makes clearly looks to the future. By bringing together the foods of different cultures, it feels as if Christian is making his own attempt to bring the world together. He is informed by the past, but every creation is an attempt to imagine a new future.

Like Emerson, Christian is a craftsman. I assure you, when catering events in Los Angeles, inventing all new approaches transforms a safe meal into a courageous experiment in the culinary arts. I have watched how hard Christian works, and I know that creating as he does requires both strength and courage.

Emerson and Christian personify the elegance of workmanship. Everyone I know envies their outcomes. It would be easy to conclude that who they are and what they have accomplished are simply the result of their rare talent. I know I would be the first to acknowledge that their talent is rare. I think it would do them a disservice to not also affirm how rare their commitment is to hard work.

We have seen far too many people publicly fail because their talent was greater than their character. Could there be a more poignant reminder of this reality than the life and career of Lance Armstrong? The winner of seven Tour de France titles and perhaps the most iconic name in the history of cycling, he was stripped of his titles because he chose not to live strong. Remember, craft means strength. If we are to live strong, we must ensure we have the strength of character to make our lives into our greatest works of art. Moments of greatness are far more appealing than a lifetime of faithfulness, but it is only through a lifetime of faithfulness—a lifetime of integrity, in which we have chosen to be strong and courageous— that we will look back and realize that our lives have become masterpieces.

Have you ever had a moment when you knew you were awesome? I know you are not supposed to say that, but have you ever thought it? You know, that moment when everything just came together. You were in perfect form. Some athletes call it "the zone"; in other disciplines, they call it "finding your flow." As a speaker, it's the moment when you don't even have to think. The words seemingly form themselves.

More often than not, that moment comes as a great surprise—that moment when you can't miss from the three-point line; that moment when you are teaching your eighth graders and you have them mesmerized, even though the subject is French history; that moment when no matter what question your antagonistic audience asks you, the answers roll off your lips as if you were Socrates; that moment when no math problem is too complex; that moment when you know exactly what to buy your wife for your anniversary; that moment when you have such clarity that the entire universe makes sense to you; that moment when you are awesome—and then you lose it. It only lasts a couple of minutes. The problem is you don't know how you got there and you have no idea how to get back. But those five minutes of greatness will haunt you the rest of your life. The loss will also mislead you. You'll spend your life trying to find the zone, get back your groove, step into your flow—and all the while what you experienced was a glimpse of the person you could become if you disciplined yourself to live at your highest level of execution. There's something wonderful about a moment when you express your best work.

Our potential future has a curious way of impinging on our present. Those moments when we are at our best open a window into the person we could become every single day for the rest of our lives. This is true not only for our talent but also for our character. Have you ever had a moment when not only were you awesome, but you were a really genuinely awesome person? You can't say it because that would ruin it, but you were really kind, humble, generous, thoughtful. It was the best *you* you had ever seen. Have you ever in a sense risen above the person you were and for at least a few moments become the person you only imagined yourself to be?

Sometimes it happens in reverse: we have five minutes of the worst of us. Usually we explain it with phrases like "I don't know what got into me" or "I just wasn't myself" or "Could we just forget what just happened?" but those moments are also windows into our future. If we're not careful, this momentary pause when we saw the worst of ourselves could become the person we wake up to every day. Without intervention, all of us have the potential to become the worst expression of ourselves. We must choose who we become.

But back to our most awesome self. Think about those five minutes—that moment where you were the ideal you. Think about what you would look like if those five minutes expanded into your life. Think about what your future would look like. Think about how the world would be better, how it would change your relationships, how it would change your life if you paid the price to become you at your best.

It is important to identify these "five minutes of greatness" because they can be windows into your future self. If you reflect on what brought you to this moment, you can begin to develop a strategy for living continuously in that sweet spot. Think about the conditions that surrounded you when you were at your best. Reflect on the condition of your internal world in those moments when you surprised yourself. Take time to relive those moments, working them deeply into your mental muscle memory so that you build patterns of excellence in your life. A life well lived is the sum total of a vast number of moments lived well.

The craftsman understands that beauty and excellence are found in the details. When it comes to
making our lives into works of art, the details are
formed by how we choose to live day by day, hour
by hour, minute by minute. The artisan understands
that the journey is marked by steps. This is the journey of the craftsman, to recognize that art has in its
universe words like *creativity, inspiration, beauty,* and
imagination, but in that same universe are words like
perseverance, resilience, tenacity, and *discipline.* We
want our lives to be works of art, but we don't want
the work to take a lifetime. And really how long does
it take to make our lives works of art?

Art becomes a craft when inspiration is expressed
in detail. Most people who describe themselves as visionaries are actually saying something quite different. They are abdicating their responsibility for the
details. Details matter. The more someone or something matters to us, the more the details relating to
them matter to us.

I have been married to Kim for twenty-nine years,
and believe me—the details matter. Big details like
birthdays and anniversaries matter. If a marriage is
going to last for thirty years, you can't just be a big-
picture guy. The beauty is in the details. The more I
grow to love Kim, the more I come to understand her. I
don't see her as simply one person among many. Love
provides me with so many details about what makes

her happy and what makes her feel most alive. When someone creates out of love, it is visible in the details. When something matters to us, the details matter.

Anyone who has taken time to read through the Hebrew Scriptures has to be struck by how unbelievably detailed God is when he gets involved in the creative process. He doesn't simply tell Noah to build a ship; he gives him details of how the ark should be constructed. He doesn't simply tell Solomon to build a temple; he lays out the details of how that temple is to be designed and built. God's process of creation involved meticulous attention to detail, including selection of the clay from which he formed man before the intimate act of breathing life into him.

We are to be guardians of the ideal, the process, and the details. There's an old adage that the devil is in the details, but the artisan understands that when life is a work of art, when we value our craft, when we embrace the elegance of workmanship, it is in the details that we experience the divine.

Moving the dream into the details is the true art of craftsmanship. It is here that we move into the tension of creation and refinement. It's easy to dream but too easy and too tempting to become lost in our dreams. It is too easy to allow our dreams to become an escape from life rather than fuel for life.

In our dreams there is no risk. This is where the creative act is vastly different from a dream. The creative act requires courage and demands action. The creative act moves us from ideation to implementation. If imagination keeps our universe ever expanding, creation holds the universe together. As creation reminds us, vision and details are not mutually exclusive.

As "big-picture" as the universe is, it is also a study in meticulous attention to detail. Here we are all called to be craftsmen. We are to work at our crafts as our expression of worship, never settling for anything less than mastery. Here we are often confused and misled. We often confuse genius with mastery. Genius is a gift we are given; mastery is the stewardship of our gifts. Our gifts and talents are the fireworks, but our commitment to mastery is the fire. Often genius is the terrain of the young, but mastery is a gift acquired only with time and hard work.

It was Michelangelo who said, "If people knew how hard I worked to get my mastery, it wouldn't seem so wonderful at all." I am certain this is why the designation *craftsman* wasn't as well received as that of *artisan* at Mosaic. To be called an artist feels like you are telling me I have talent; to be called a craftsman sounds like you are describing me as a hard worker. We believe that one is about essence and the other about effort. Can you imagine what our lives would be if we valued both? Only when we realize that craft is rooted in character can we begin the journey to mastery. In the discipline that comes from passion, we find our way to mastery.

Henri Matisse once said of his process, "An artist must possess nature. He must identify himself with her rhythm, by efforts that will prepare the mastery which will later enable him to express himself in his own language." The mastery of our craft should be paramount, for without it we will never have the language to tell the full story of our lives. To leave our gifts and talents unmastered and undeveloped is to leave unwrapped precious treasures entrusted to us.

We have no control over the gifts and talents given to us, but we have every responsibility for their stewardship. This is our creative act; this is our work as an artisan; this is our craft. There is only one you, just as there is only one me. Each of us is unique and original. Each of us has been given all the materials necessary for our lives to become works of art. For this very reason, because of all that has been placed within us, it is both our duty and our privilege to give ourselves and our lives the time and attention they deserve. The craftsman is patient and deliberative when it comes to his life as a work of art. The masterpiece takes time—it takes a lifetime.

Canvas

The Context of Art

When I was studying art in college, we were forced at times to use particular mediums. Whether it was pen and ink or pastels or charcoals, whether we were instructed to work with clay or other unexpected materials, the challenge was always trying to translate what we saw in our imagination using the medium provided. It was a painful exercise in coming face-to-face with reality. Every time we engaged a new medium, I discovered new limitations. I discovered both how limiting the materials were and how limited I was with the materials.

There are few things as humbling as those moments when the classroom turns into a gallery, when your work product is a declaration of how little can be done with a particular medium, even as a nearby work demonstrates the limitless possibilities that come when those same materials are informed by imagination, talent, and skill. If I remember correctly, one of the questions I asked most was, "How did you do that?" I remember asking that of a little boy when he drew a cat that actually looked like a cat. I was astonished by his talent and asked him quite spontaneously, "How did you do that?" He looked at me as if it was a strange question and responded, "I just looked at the cat and drew what I saw." It's that easy, you know—except that it's not.

Every creative endeavor becomes a realization of both how limited and how unlimited we are. Regardless of medium, when imagination, talent, and skill are infused into the artistic process, the work product seems to promise almost boundless possibility. Yet the medium can also be a cruel reminder of how limited we are.

One of the great misconceptions about creativity is that it only exists where there are no rules, no boundaries, and no limitations. Often people who find it difficult to express their true creativity blame external forces. They point to rules and boundaries and limitations as the reasons their creativity has not flourished. They become convinced that creativity blooms only when we are free of boundaries. Yet this understanding of creativity is exactly wrong. The artist always has a canvas. There is always a context for art.

Every medium carries within itself inherent limitations, and every artist also comes with limitations. True creativity is not the outflow of a world without boundaries. The creative act is the genius of unleashing untapped potential and unseen beauty within the constraints and boundaries of the medium from which we choose to create. Creativity not only happens within boundaries and limitations, but in fact it is dependent on those limitations. The true artist sees boundaries not as the materials denied to us but as the material that allows us to harness and focus our full creative potential. There are things we can do with clay that we cannot do with stone. There are different rules of engagement when our medium of choice is wood and when our medium is metal.

Part of the artistic process is understanding the rules under which mediums express themselves and learning how to work within them so as to materialize your imagination through them. The canvas informs the creative act. This may be painful for a person who values creative freedom. Our creativity is not in conflict with boundaries but must work with them. To break free of the limits of any medium, we must first embrace them.

All colors are nuanced expressions of three primary colors. Our creative capacity to mix these colors and create through unexpected hues seems unlimited, but in the end it all comes back to blue, red, and yellow. We can spend our lives lamenting that there are only three primary colors, or we can spend our lives imagining and mixing those three and beautifully defying the limitations.

We could abandon painting and move to music so that we might find more freedom, but here once again the limitations are clear—at best you get only twelve notes in the chromatic scale. We could see it as a vicious cycle: do, re, mi, fa, so, la, ti, and then back to do, just an octave higher. Not Mozart, Beethoven, John Lennon, or Bon Iver get to add a thirteenth or fourteenth note into the mix. Creativity isn't about finding the thirteenth note; it is about arranging twelve notes in a way the world has never experienced before.

Could anyone's work be more different than that of Frank Gehry, Frank Lloyd Wright, and Antoni Gaudi? In the end, all three are defined by the same three simple expressions—circles, triangles, and squares. From the time of Michelangelo to our most modernist expressions of architecture, everything is human creativity expressed through curves, angles, and lines.

If creativity exists only where there are no boundaries, then some of our most creative minds wasted their time in architecture. Not only is their medium profoundly limited, but their environment is also limited. Architects are not measured by their ability to simply create beautiful things; their work must be functional as well. They must contend with the harsh realities of gravity, topography, and environmental conditions. Yet if we ever have the privilege of walking into one of their buildings, the experience might cause us to believe in magic. We have to wonder how in the world these exquisite works of art are also some of the most trustworthy and resilient structures the world has ever known.

On a lighter note, we see the same dynamic when it comes to the culinary arts. Historically we have known four flavors—bitter, sweet, salty, and sour. Every meal we have ever eaten and every flavor we have ever experienced is expressive of one or a combination of these. Only recently have we identified the existence of a fifth flavor detectable by human taste, called umami. It is ironic that while we have somewhere between two thousand and five thousand taste buds located on the back and front of our tongues, there are only five sensations of taste that we can experience. Yet any foodie knows that those five taste sensations can be combined to create an endless number of extraordinary experiences.

The perceived limitation is in the medium, but the actual limitation is in the artist. Everyone begins with the same material; it's what we do with the material that matters. It's what we can do with the material that distinguishes the mundane from the unique. We aren't limited because we have limitations; we are limited because we haven't embraced them. The canvas is the context for all creativity. What makes you a chef is what you do with those five flavors; what makes you a musician is what you do with those twelve notes; what makes you a painter is what you do with those three colors; what makes you an architect is what you do with those three shapes; what makes you an artist is what you do with the material you have been given with which to create.

My hero as a kid was my uncle Richard. He was more like an older brother than an uncle. Back in El Salvador, Richard was our hero. He was a musician and an artist, the lead singer of a popular Central American band called the Mustangs, which played Spanish rock and roll. I still remember him wearing a fake mustache to try to look as old as the other band members. Throughout the day, random girls called our home hoping to talk with our own rock and roll star. And Richard was also a martial arts expert. Not only was he an artist, but he was a man's man, the kind of guy who could play the guitar and then break bricks with his hand. But there was something about

Richard that went far deeper than the cool. He was also intensely compassionate and proved to be a true humanitarian. Our modest house in San Salvador became a haven for the poor. It was impossible for Richard to ever turn anyone away. He was always giving food or whatever was available to those who had greater need.

He was also a hero to me personally. I had the greatest grandmother in the world. Mami Finita was like an angel to us—except when we made her mad. She wielded a belt like an old-time cowboy wrangling the wild mustangs into the stable. I can't even remember how many times Richard defended me and my brother Alex from our grandmother when she had had more than enough. I still vividly remember her saying, "If you won't let me hit them, then I'm just going to hit you." At the age of five, we were more than willing to hide behind Richard and let Mami take it out on him.

Years later, Richard worked in Madrid, where he focused on bringing international development to developing countries. Before that, he worked in the dangerous arena of bringing freedom to the poor and standing against the injustice and oppression wielded by those in positions of power. I am sure there are many things about my uncle Richard that I did not know and that would make him seem more than human, but for me he was a canvas of what it meant to be a man. He was a warrior poet, humane and heroic, kind and strong. More than once he served as inspiration for the person I hoped I would become. Whether Richard realized it or not, he was not only making his life his own work of art, but he was painting on the canvas of my soul as well. So much of who I imagined I could become I first saw in him. The colors we use to paint our own lives splash all over the souls of those who are close to us.

Humanity is our most important canvas, our most important medium. As we strive to make our lives our most meaningful works of art, we quickly discover that our humanity is both our gift and our curse. The bigger we dream, the greater we risk. The more we want to create, the more we become aware of our limitations, our boundaries, and our deficiencies. It is easy, then, to look at other people's lives and wonder why they do not have the same deficits. It is easy to convince ourselves that successful people are simply made from different material than we are. It's easier to believe that creative people are simply different rather than to believe they are the same but choose to live differently.

Regardless, we each have a place where we are supposed to stand, a place where we are intended to create, a context in which we are to live out our lives and turn them into masterpieces. The challenge is that the longer we fail to fulfill this creative intent, the more we become aware of our limitations and lose touch with our possibilities. This tension can be very subtle. We can live our lives in such a way that outside observers marvel at what we've created while we drown in our own emptiness. Our lives can be marked by achievement and success and even celebrity, and yet our souls remain unfulfilled, unsatisfied, and unawakened. There's nothing more frustrating than creating out of a vacuum, and nothing more debilitating than allowing ourselves to be defined by our limitations. When we find ourselves living a life that is unsatisfying and unfulfilling, we begin to believe that we cannot create a life worth living, that the obstacles keeping us from that life are beyond our control.

Growing up, I never felt talented. I felt that when God cut the canvas, he was unfairly frugal—perhaps even stingy—when it came to me. My brother got a lot of canvas—he was supersmart, supertalented, superpopular. I can't even begin to describe the immense talent, intelligence, and capacity in my sisters. All around me was proof that something went terribly wrong with my genes. All my cousins were doctors, and every family member seemed to be multilingual and multitalented. I spent the first twenty years of my life overwhelmed by the sad state of affairs and the cruel injustice of how talent is disbursed in the universe.

I remember the first time we saw the *Mona Lisa*. It was at the request of my daughter Mariah. She ran through the Louvre as if nothing mattered except finding that one painting. I don't know what I was expecting, but I was definitely expecting more. Have you ever seen the *Mona Lisa* up close? It's really, really small. Framed, it's about 31 by 21—inches, that is. I don't know if you can imagine those dimensions, but you could pretty much put it on the back of a T-shirt. I had to wonder if da Vinci was rationing that day or if canvas was somehow a rare commodity. I mean, if you're going to make a masterpiece, couldn't you spare some extra canvas? Still, Mariah was not disappointed. Its beauty and elegance escaped the narrow limits of the frame and easily traveled into the depths of her soul.

Great art is not limited to its canvas any more than it is limited by its medium. Great art transcends boundaries and travels in the infinite space of the human soul. All around us, there are examples of artists realizing extraordinary creative potential by embracing limitations and understanding that those limitations do not hinder the creative process but in fact become conduits of our most creative selves.

Phil Hansen showed tremendous promise in extreme pointillism, until his intense style caused a tremor to develop in his hand while he was in art school. He was later diagnosed with severe nerve damage. This left him devastated, and he dropped out and gave up on what was once a promising career. Everything changed when a neurologist suggested he "embrace the shake." The change of perspective was a turning point in Hansen's life, sending him on a quest that has led to new and extraordinary approaches in the field of art. Hansen embraces his personal limitations and seemingly challenges our perceptions of universal limitations. Using unconventional materials such as bananas, matches, and dandelion puffs, and unconventional canvases, such as bandages and even his own body, he merges materials and canvases into the medium of film and time, creating art that is both image and movement. Hansen's art is a reminder that our limitations can become the cutting edge of creation.

Joshua Prager is a brilliant journalist and storyteller who has for a decade expressed his voice as a writer for *The Wall Street Journal.* I had the pleasure of hearing him speak at the world-renowned TED conference. I was mesmerized as he spoke, hearing his personal story and his reminder that our limitations are often not what we perceive them to be. In 1990, a bus accident in Jerusalem left him a hemiplegic at the age of nineteen. Watching him as he struggled to walk onto the platform and then mesmerized us through his prowess with language was a reminder that limitations are often perceptions and not realities. It all depends on how we allow those limitations to restrain us or refocus us. Certainly paralysis brought dramatic changes to his life, ending possibilities no one would want to lose, yet somehow even paralysis could not prevent him from unleashing his extraordinary genius. I sat there wondering if in fact the tragic end of so many possibilities was not the essential context necessary to such extraordinary thoughtfulness.

Eleanor Longden was diagnosed as schizophrenic, which is a clinical way of saying someone is crazy. And believe me, I know what it's like to be thrown into a box where you are defined by your struggles rather than by your strengths. While all of us are a bit neurotic, the diagnosis of schizophrenia rarely leaves a person with a hopeful ending. Yet Eleanor refused to allow herself to be defined by what was seen as an insurmountable psychological limitation. She showed that hearing voices in her head was not proof of schizophrenia but "a creative and genius survival strategy." For Longden, hearing voices in her head was a "sane reaction to insane circumstances." Longden began her psychiatric journey as a patient long before earning a bachelor of science and a master's in science and psychology from the University of Leeds in England. Today the same person who was once misdiagnosed with schizophrenia is studying for her doctorate in the same field that once condemned her as a schizophrenic. She took what others would consider a debilitating limitation and turned it into a platform for creativity and genius. Longden understood that the complex psychological trauma often described as schizophrenia was in fact a creative and ingenious survival strategy. She saw it "not as an abstract symptom of illness to be endured, but a complex, significant and meaningful experience to be explored."

As I listened to these extraordinary individuals at the TED conference, I was reminded that those who change the world do so not because they are free of the limitations that keep us from achieving our full capacity, but because they embrace those limitations and allow them to be the conduit of unleashing their most creative selves.

It is curious that the Ten Commandments have been used to prove that God wants to limit our freedom. It is true that the driving narrative within the commandments is built on the phrase *do not*. It's much less appealing to be told what not to do than to be inspired about what we should do. Still, regardless of the language of these commands, the intention is clearly not to limit human freedom but to protect it. Often I hear the commandments used as proof that God is way too demanding or even that religion is only a mechanism to control people and limit their enjoyment of life. I didn't grow up with the Ten Commandments, so I must admit being surprised at first that the arguments against them seemed unfair and in fact unwarranted. The Ten Commandments are not an ambitious set of rules. They can in no way be described as an appeal to human ideals.

The Ten Commandments establish what I described in my first book, *An Unstoppable Force,* as the minimal standard for living a humane life. What exactly is ambitious about a command that says, "Do not steal" or "Do not kill" or "Do not bear false witness"? These are not about inspiring. They are not appeals to our nobility but rather attempts to keep us from crawling lower than we had already managed to do up to that time.

Maybe I'm an idealist, but we shouldn't have to ask each other not to kill each other or steal from each other or lie to each other. Imagine a world where everyone lived beneath these boundaries. Imagine a world where people killed when they were angry or stole what someone else had when they wanted it or lied to both friends and enemies when it served their purposes. I quickly realized that the Ten Commandments were not a high bar calling us to an extraordinary expression of being human, but the lowest bar possible, pleading with us to reclaim our humanity.

In fact, the Ten Commandments provide a perfect example of why boundaries are essential for freedom and creativity to find their greatest expression. When we are committed to not stealing, we have to commit ourselves to creating. Often that's a code word for work. When we resolve to never lie again, the commitment to telling the truth drives us to live a life that is trustworthy. When we make a commitment to never kill, we have to deal with our anger issues and learn the power of forgiveness.

The Ten Commandments not only do not restrict human freedom; they protect human freedom. Instead of limiting human creativity, they provide the context from which we become our most creative selves. Even the God of the Scriptures embraces limitations, which is kind of unexpected for a God who is all-powerful, all-knowing, and all-present. Why embrace limitations when the context for your creativity is the omnis? Yet the creative act has within it inherent limitations. The moment we create, we establish boundaries and limitations.

The first creative act described in the Scriptures, "Let there be light," has no observable limitations. But once God creates light, new rules come into play. This becomes apparent in the next movements of his creative act. He creates the universe, and the universe has rules. In that universe, there are galaxies and solar systems, and those bodies contain their own rules. The solar system has rules specific to this planet we know as Earth—the design of the sun, the relationship and distance between Earth and the sun, as well as Earth's revolution and rotation. Boundaries are set into place—from the rules of gravity to the chemicals to the specific formulas that create water and atmosphere.

What we discover is that the closer the creative process comes to creating life, the more rules, boundaries, and limitations there actually are. In that sense, there are fewer rules on Mars than there are on Earth, just as there's less life on the red planet than there is on the blue planet. The rules become more intricate and the context more complex as God heightens his creative expression. When he creates the birds of the air and the fish of the sea and the animals that walk the earth, the boundaries are clearly established—each species with its own limitations, each creative act with its own rules, gills to survive in water, wings to travel the air.

Yet the integrity of the universe is the context in which creativity is best expressed. The canvas does not limit God's creativity but rather celebrates it. The elegant complexity of creation is a beautiful reminder that the creative mind is a disciplined mind, that the creative act is not a struggle to be free of limitations but a demonstration that when we embrace our limitations, creativity has no boundaries.

The culminating act in Genesis 1 is the creation of humanity. In a very real sense, the earlier creative acts were far less limiting than God's final act. When energy is transformed into matter, there are endless possibilities of how that could play out. But in this final creative act, the creation of the first man, there is far more context and thus the creative process is more complex. The canvas is smaller, so the work of art has to be even more detailed. The creation of man could not be based on whim or boundless imagination. The man had to fit the material already created. God took clay from the earth, material that already existed, and created a living being who had to fit the detailed intricacies of the living system he had already created. Creating man was far more complex than creating light. Creating humanity in the image of himself was a far greater creative act than even creating the universe with all its complexity and wonder.

In some ways, we could say that God painted himself into a corner. When God created us, he didn't have a lot of options. We had to be able to breathe oxygen; we had to be able to drink water; we had to be able to eat what the earth provided; we had to fit the canvas. A lesser artist would have felt paralyzed, incapable of completing this masterpiece. For God, though, the opposite was true. He reveled in the challenge. He took great pleasure in creating a creature whose material is the substance of the earth and whose essence is the image of God. And yes, this is a wonderful reminder that we are a work of art, and the limitations that often lead us to conclude that we're only human should move us to celebrate that we are in fact incredibly human.

This is especially powerful when we realize that we are God's medium of choice. Because the created order reflects the majesty of God and declares his glory, nothing in the universe is more finely crafted or better designed for divine purpose than a human being. You are God's preferred medium to express himself and reveal himself. God loves working through people. Talk about choosing a limitation— when we think that God would choose to step into human history and reveal himself as a man, it is hard to imagine a more limiting creative choice for God than becoming human.

Yet here we see that God's most creative act, rescuing all humanity, could be accomplished only when he emptied himself of his limitlessness and took on the limitations of being human. For the singular act that brought salvation to the world, God chose what for him must have seemed the smallest of canvases and the most common of materials. To do his greatest work, he embraced his greatest limitations. Above all, he understood that the intention of the art determines the medium that must be chosen. To save humanity, he would need to become a man; to conquer death, he would need to be crucified; to bring us back to life, he would need to be resurrected; to heal our wounds, he would need to be wounded; to free us from ourselves, he would need to become our prisoner.

The artisan soul understands that if our lives are to be our masterpieces and if life itself is our most creative act, then we must embrace life as a canvas and recognize that the medium we have chosen (or haven't chosen) comes with boundaries and limitations and that these boundaries are not to be despised but to be embraced. For the finished product to reflect our imagination, we must choose our notes carefully, mix our colors skillfully, and respect how the medium informs the process so that we can achieve our most creative outcome. Beauty is not the expression of a universe void of principles; beauty is the masterful expression of creativity despite constraints.

When I was a young boy, I would sneak out of bed after my parents went to sleep, turn on our twelve-inch TV set at the lowest volume, and watch endless episodes of *The Twilight Zone* and *Night Gallery*. I was a huge Rod Serling fan. In 1970, Rod Serling came out with *Night Gallery*, the follow-up to his timeless *Twilight Zone*. Whereas *The Twilight Zone* was an exploration of science fiction, *Night Gallery* focused on opening the dark closets in the human soul. One particular story has stayed with me over the years. Josef

Strobe is a Nazi war criminal hiding out in South America—Argentina, I imagine. In spite of his cruel and evil past, his deepest longing is simply to be a fisherman. His history haunts him, forcing him to live in a world that is dingy and bleak, a vivid contrast to his opulent life while in power. Always afraid of being caught and constantly on the move, he is a different kind of prisoner than those comrades who were captured years before and condemned for their crimes against humanity.

He stands in front of a beautiful painting of a fisherman in a small boat drifting serenely on a still mountain lake, imagining himself as the man in the boat, free from all the problems that he has created for himself. Josef is drawn to the painting over and over again. He asks a forgiving God to give him another chance, a chance to survive, but in truth he is asking God to absolve him from his sins while he abdicates all responsibility for his actions.

As he dreams of being the man in the painting, he wonders if, by concentrating all his mind and all his desire, he could enter that picture, leaving behind the life he has created to enter a life he could only dream of. It's clear, though, that Josef has never known contrition. In the midst of his anguish, he runs across a Holocaust survivor who recognizes him as a former guard. Josef kills the Jewish man and tries to escape by leaving town.

Instead, he is captured after some tense moments. He escapes and sneaks back into the museum, rushing toward the painting that holds the world he longs to live in. It is dark not only from the lack of light but from the ominous presence of the moment. He prays to God to allow him to enter into the painting, then suddenly disappears. Rushing into the room seconds later, a security guard and a museum official hear muted screams where Josef had stood. The picture of the mountain lake is gone, and the curator explains that the painting of the mountain lake was a loaner. In its place hangs the image of a man crucified in a concentration camp. Slowly the camera scans to the picture, and we realize that Josef has taken the place of the person who was crucified. In a twist of irony, Josef Strobe has found his way back to the world he created.

This narrative is a stark reminder that often the life we live is not at all a reflection of the life we long for. We may not get to choose the canvas, but we can choose the painting. We live in a multidimensional reality, and for the most part we all work with the same material. Objects have height, length, and width, the dimensions to create depth. In some way or another, our art is bounded by these realities. But what happens inside these three dimensions is apparently endless in its expression.

When it comes to life, there are similar dimensions we use to create depth. The height, length, and width of the art of life are our relationships, accomplishments, and well-being. If you want to assess how your artistic expression is progressing, simply evaluate these three aspects of your life. In the greatest expressions of a life lived as a work of art, we find beauty and artistry in our relationships. The artisan soul knows that everything begins here. We cannot live our lives as works of art and not hold people as our highest value. We humans are designed for relationship and find our greatest fulfillment in intimacy.

No single attribute creates more beauty in the world than a life lived out of love. Imagine how the world would be different if each of us left every person we ever met better than we found them. Imagine a world where love was the rule, where love was the boundary, where it was unthinkable to violate this principle: *love your neighbor as yourself.* It is not incidental that when Jesus was asked, "What must I do to inherit eternal life?" his response was, "Love." "Love the Lord your God with all your heart, and with all your soul, and with all your strength, and with all your mind; and love your neighbor as yourself" (Luke 10:27). Whatever else we may accomplish in our lives, if we neglect this arena, if we diminish the importance of human relationships, if we live our lives for any lesser principle than the principle of love, our lives will not be our greatest works of art. Love creates a beautiful life. As an artist, you must never forget that your principal canvas in life is relationships.

The second dimension of our canvas is accomplishments. Just as we are all created to belong, we're all equally driven to become. The human spirit is designed for progress. In that sense, we are created to create. In an ideal world, this creative energy is to be used to create the good and the beautiful and the true. If in relationships we are to leave each person better than we found them, in our accomplishments we should leave the world better than we found it.

The romantic imagines what his life would look like if love always prevailed, but our romantic fantasies do not end there. It's inherent to the human spirit to imagine what our lives would look like if we fulfilled our greatest potential. Whatever language we use to describe it, we all have a sense of destiny, or at the very least we long to find meaning in our lives. Our lives will become our greatest works of art not only when our relationships are a beautiful expression of love, acceptance, and intimacy, but when we have a deep sense of purpose that produces accomplishments that express, for us, success and significance.

But just as height and length need width to create depth, so the human experience needs a third dimension as it becomes a work of art. Beyond relationships and accomplishments is the arena of well-being. If relationships express how we treat others and accomplishments express our stewardship over our talent, then well-being reflects how we have cared for the health of our soul.

I think it would be fair to say that all of us, as we become more self-aware, become more aware of our own neurosis. The healthier we become, the more clearly we see our imperfections, inadequacies, and faults. Well-being is not a journey toward perfection, but a journey toward wholeness. Well-being is not a destination; it is the realization that the journey itself brings fulfillment and even creates happiness.

It has been popular to diminish the importance of happiness and focus on the more substantial value of joy. Happiness has been seen as a superficial emotion—entirely dependent on our circumstances—while joy is understood as a more substantive state, being akin to inner peace or contentment. I would never diminish the significance of joy, but I think it is equally vital to reflect on the critical importance of happiness. Somewhere in the Dark Ages, we became convinced that spirituality and happiness were mutually exclusive and that happiness was the playground of children and joy the best adults can hope for. After five decades of living and interacting with thousands upon thousands of individuals across the world, I can tell you that there is an undeniable relationship between happiness and resilience. People who enjoy life make life more enjoyable for others. It's strange, but one can be profoundly loved and still lack the wholeness to experience that love. One can be unimaginably accomplished and not be able to enjoy the benefit of that success due to a lack of personal well-being. Yet well-being is often neglected by the artisan. Far too often they imagine beauty and leave it to the ideal, while passively accepting that tragedy is the only human experience they will ever know.

All three of these dimensions demand engagement if our lives are to have the depth demanded by the masterpiece we long to create.

I am reminded of the simple words in the Scriptures, "Do this and you will live" (Luke 10:28). Jesus's echo of that promise is, "I have come that they may have life, and have it to the full" (John 10:10). Clearly God does not feel limited by the human canvas. He is more than certain that he can work with the material of our broken humanity to create a life that is nothing less than divinely inspired.

The question is not, "Who are you?" That's simply the result of taking time to identify the material. The question is, "Who will you decide to become?" That's the measure of the artisan soul. The canvas is only the context for the creative act.

Masterpiece

A New Humanity

I mentioned Emerson in an earlier chapter. During the writing of this book, Emerson and his wife Christina have been guests in our home. They are the Latin version of Prince Charming and Snow White—beautiful in every way. Emerson and I not only work together but have become good friends. I admire him both as an artist and as a person. To experience Emerson is to experience a beautiful combination of strength and gentleness. He is that rare combination of ridiculous talent merged with unexpected humility. You can only imagine the surprise I felt when he shared with me that he was an ex-convict. It seemed like he was telling someone else's story. Or if it was him, it had to be in another life.

He explained how he met a girl when he was sixteen and fell in love. He was a person of deep faith who felt as if his life was coming together like a work of art. After they were engaged, the love of his life began showing signs of sickness. Though Emerson knew something was wrong, his fiancée's family kept hidden that she had been diagnosed with cancer. Though Emerson was fully committed to her, she called off the wedding a week before the ceremony. He was devastated. This led to the end of his faith and the beginning of a life that would end his freedom.

Through distant relatives, Emerson got involved in a San Diego drug cartel. For the next two and a half years, Emerson ran drugs and money for the cartel, until at the age of twenty-four, he was caught with 7.6 kilos of cocaine, worth $230,000. Under normal circumstances, this crime would garner a sentence of seventeen years in a federal penitentiary. Because he tried to make amends, Emerson's sentence was reduced to five years. A month before he went to prison, he met Christina, who would later become his wife. Emerson and Christina were married on

November 3, 2007. Today they live in Los Angeles, where Christina works for a film company and Emerson is on the leadership team at Mosaic in Hollywood.

Michelangelo once said, "In every block of marble I see a statue as plain as though it stood before me, shaped and perfect in attitude and action. I have only to hew away the rough walls that imprison the lovely apparition to reveal it to the other eyes as mine see it." Emerson was a work of art trapped inside a block of marble. That's the beauty of the masterpiece of our lives. God chips away at the rough walls that imprison us until the beautiful emerges.

Remember, the only world we can create is the one that reflects our soul. All art is an extension of ourselves. That may be in its simplest definition what art is and has always been. Art is an expression of the human need to create. As artisans, our story tells the story of all of us. When art is both universal and intimate, it becomes transcendent. We find ourselves in the masterpiece. It tells our story and reveals our hidden selves. The masterpiece both exposes us and inspires us. It is both authentic and idealistic. It touches both our pain and our hope. Artists do not paint simply for themselves. Art is stewardship of the human story and the great quest to come. It only finds its meaning when it resonates with, reveals, and re-creates the soul.

It is the same with our lives. When a life is a work of art, it is always more than simply an expression of ourselves. Life becomes a work of art when we live it not for ourselves but for others. We live and tell our story, and through it we carry the hope of the world. The masterpiece is a life lived with courage and faith, with integrity and intention, with love and passion. We know we've seen a work of art when a life inspires us to be more—to live more fully and authentically.

It is here that I find Jesus to be my greatest inspiration. He points me not only to the divine but, even more profoundly, to what it means to be fully human. His life was a masterpiece—a subtle, elegant, and brilliant work of art. His was a life painted with light and vivid color. And that light and color were profoundly contrasted with the harsh, dark background of hate, betrayal, and suffering. Yet in the midst of it all, he never failed to emanate grace and truth. To engage the life of Christ is to watch an artist at work. Through his sacrifice, he turned the cross, that barbaric instrument of death, into a symbol of beauty and hope.

Great art not only tells the truth but elevates the human spirit by pointing to beauty and hope. In this sense, great art paints a picture of human ideals. It carries within it the story of the best of us interwoven into the story of any and every art form. It is not only the story we know to be true, but the story we hope is true. Great art inspires us to become our most noble selves. It inspires us to greater courage, to greater sacrifice. Great art reminds us that in the midst of tragedy there is always beauty. The masterpiece refuses to leave us in the mundane and demands that the human spirit soar to a divine level. If art exists to remind us that we have a soul, the masterpiece is a glimpse into its divine nature. There is a difference between timely art that brings us pleasure for a moment and timeless art that points us to eternity, reminding us of the uniqueness of being human and the power that comes in our shared experiences.

Have you ever trusted someone untrustworthy with a particular responsibility and later said to yourself, "You knew what he was. What did you expect from him?" Intuitively we all know that the work we receive from a person is an extension of who that person is.

This reminds me of Jesus's first miracle. If his closing act was the Resurrection, I find it incredibly odd that his opening act was to turn water into wine. I mean, it's kind of underwhelming. When you heal a leper, the importance is self-explanatory. The drama of saying to a paralytic, "Pick up your mat and walk" (John 5:8), is awe inspiring. I don't imagine Jesus actually had a limit on how many miracles he could perform while he was here on earth, but we can be certain that he had limited time. It seems strange to waste a miracle on turning water to wine.

This is how Jesus chose to introduce himself to the world. It all begins at a wedding. A celebration is taking place. I imagine there was dancing and drinking and laughter. It is nice to know that Jesus spent time enjoying experiences like this. The curious part is being clearly unprepared for either the number of people who joined them in the celebration or the volume of alcohol they were going to consume.

Mary, the mother of Jesus, comes and informs him that they are out of wine. I know it's Jesus's mother, but this request seems out of line. Even Jesus seems irritated by her request. His mother, like every mother in the world, ignores his resistance and acts as if he has every intention of fulfilling her request. But it really isn't Jesus's problem, and in any case, solving the problem doesn't fix anything in the world—not even for a moment. At the very best, all it does is add a bit more joy and celebration for a few people in an obscure part of the planet. Surely God has more important concerns than our enjoyment of life. But it's not outside God's intention or his desire to meet us in the common places of everyday life. And it's possible that the same God who makes the blind see finds equal pleasure in increasing our happiness. But it's what happens in the midst of the miracle that is critical for this particular part of this artistic process.

Jesus takes the six stone water jars used by the Jews for their ceremonial washing, each of which holds from twenty to thirty gallons, and has the servants fill the jars with water. After that, he tells them to draw some out and take it to the master of the banquet. The master of the banquet tastes the water that was turned into wine. He has no idea where it came from, though the servants, we are told, know exactly what happened. The master of ceremonies calls the bridegroom aside and says, "Everyone brings out the choice wine first and then the cheaper wine after the guests have had too much to drink; but you have saved the best till now" (John 2:10).

There is so much nuance in this moment. Clearly, an expected part of the culture was to serve your best up front while people were still sober, then bring out the cheap stuff later, when people were too drunk to notice the difference. This approach was quite the opposite of how Jesus engaged the moment. He produced for them, out of nothing but water, the best wine they had ever tasted. This detail is too nuanced to be incidental. But like we talked about earlier, a person's work product reflects his or her essence. All that can really be said is, what did you expect? What kind of wine would the Creator of the universe make after all? Can you imagine in any universe that the Creator of the entire cosmos would put his signature on anything less than the most extraordinary expression of his work? You do not speak light into existence and then create a $3 bottle of sangria.

At the conclusion of this miracle, John comments that what Jesus did in Cana of Galilee was the first of the signs by which he revealed his glory, and his disciples believed in him. Again, quite an unexpected result from such a seemingly insignificant miracle for God. It wasn't simply that Jesus turned water into wine that revealed his glory; it was that Jesus took ordinary water and turned it into exquisite wine that revealed who he really was.

Remember, art is an extension of self. Everything we create reveals who we are. The material that forms our souls is the only material we have available to us when we create. If the artisan paints with the soul, what are the colors available to us? Beavers create dams; bees create hives; ants create colonies; but humans create futures. The unique distinction of being created in the image of God is that what we create is informed by the invisible at the same time as it materializes the invisible.

When our souls are informed by human emotions that reflect the worst in us, we find ourselves creating a world that not even we ourselves would ever want to live in. When our inner world is filled with bitterness, unforgivingness, jealousy, envy, greed, and lust, then the darkness inside creates a dark world around us. But when the human spirit is shaped by the highest human virtues, such as love, kindness, goodness, joy, and gentleness, we create a beautiful world.

The greatest art is an intersection of contrasts. There is hope in the midst of pain, love in the midst of betrayal, courage in the midst of mystery. To turn our lives into masterpieces is to know both pain and healing, despair and hope, darkness and light. Our most powerful work comes when we reveal beauty in the midst of tragedy.

For all of us, part of this journey is learning how to turn the water into wine. What I love most about this particular miracle is that Jesus never had to tell them that a miracle had happened. It wasn't the spectacular nature of the transaction that indicated the divine intervention; it was the quality of the product.

This I have found to be the best metaphor for my own journey. The best description of my life is watching God time and time again turn water into wine.

We have no control over the status of our birth or the genetic configuration that makes someone a prodigy or a genius, but we all have the opportunity to step into life's circumstances and refuse to surrender to the mundane. We can bring meaning to every moment in every circumstance.

If we look at our lives and wonder why all God gave us was water, we can find solace in this: if we want to experience the wonder of turning it into wine, we have to start with water. The longer I live, the more grateful I am that I started with such low expectations about the life I would live and what I would accomplish. Even when it came to my journey of faith, the lack of expectation echoed in every room I entered. The first words I heard on the night I publicly surrendered my life to vocational ministry were my mother's, when she gave me a warm embrace, then looked me sadly in the eyes and said, "What in the world is God going to do with you?" Frankly, she only gave words to the question that was already rumbling inside my own head.

It's hard to escape the voices that let us know we are nothing but water, yet they become a point of celebration when we realize that God has special expertise in using common materials. If alchemy is the magical craft of turning common elements into precious materials, then God is certainly the alchemist of the human soul. His expertise is taking into his masterful care ordinary people who have lived broken lives, and turning our lives into nothing less than masterpieces.

Even this does not accurately describe the process. There has never been nor will there ever be a human being who could accurately be described as common material, regardless of how much evidence to the contrary our lives may have accumulated or how masterfully we've managed to make our lives as mundane and ordinary as humanly possible. This is not indicative of the material from which we come.

This year I came to know a man named Todd Younger. Todd was born in Delaware and is one of the brightest individuals I know, with a keen sense of humor. Todd was a typical toddler until the day of his sister's sixteenth birthday party, when he was left in his parents' bed to rest. Todd was later found unresponsive. Rescue CPR and emergency room hospitalization saved his life, but a reaction to two high doses of penicillin administered in the hospital rendered Todd a quadriplegic forced to spend every day until age seven in an iron lung.

The guilt and pain in his family destroyed their relationships. His mother developed crippling anxiety attacks, and his father compensated for his powerlessness to help Todd by becoming harsh and controlling and keeping everyone in a state of fear. As Todd matured, he was determined to become independent and successful. He moved from a school designed for people with severe disabilities to a public high school and later found work with Unocal and Pepsi. Although he was a quadriplegic continuously dependent on a tracheostomy tube to breathe, he nevertheless vowed never to be dependent on his family and to find a way to be self-reliant. When I asked him what motivated him, he replied, "Anger." Anger kept him alive; anger kept him moving—anger at life, anger at the world, anger at God.

This is not the Todd I know. I met Todd when he began coming to Mosaic, our community in Los Angeles. I will never forget the day he called me aside and explained that he wanted to be baptized. This would be no small task. It actually posed a serious risk to his health, but he was determined to be immersed despite his paralysis and tracheostomy. He wanted his decision to follow Christ to be public and emphatic. When I asked him why, he was very clear: "There is someone in my life that I love, and they are bound by fear. Perhaps my commitment to do this will help them be free."

Todd is a beautiful reminder that what seems like a great limitation from one vantage point can be, from a very different perspective, the material for our greatness. In that moment, all of us who had the privilege of being present were watching and experiencing a masterpiece. For us, Todd was our *Mona Lisa*.

There has never been an ordinary human being born on this planet. But while there has never been an ordinary child born on this earth, the undeniable tragedy is that most of us die after having lived painfully ordinary lives. Every child is born with his own genius, her unique creativity. Every human being is brimming with divine potential. Every one of us is born with an artisan soul. It was Picasso who said, "Every child is born an artist. The problem is staying an artist when you grow up."

When you were born, you were no ordinary child, but perhaps like so many of us you traded your uniqueness for acceptance, your genius for security. For some reason, describing someone as an artist always suggests seeing them as irresponsible. The artist is the person who refuses to take responsibility; the artist chooses to never grow up; the artist is never the guy you want your daughter to marry, unless of course he's already extremely successful, but then it's not his artistry that has won you over but his entrepreneurship, or more bluntly, his success. We all understand that putting our children's finger paintings on the refrigerator and telling them their work is amazing is supposed to be a temporary phase and that eventually they will grow out of their need to create beautiful things and be celebrated for it.

Every child is an artist. Every human being is born with all the necessary tools with which to create a work of art. I don't know what you are like now, but I know you were born with curiosity, imagination, creativity, and courage. Human development is impossible without curiosity. It's what gets babies to push themselves up against the crib and strengthen their necks until they can finally turn themselves over to see the world around them. It was curiosity that got us moving; it was curiosity that forced us to find strength to make the turn; it was our incessant curiosity that motivated us to crawl but allowed us to overcome the fear of falling until we could walk; and it was our indomitable curiosity that caused us to run from our mothers' arms toward a freedom filled with mystery and danger.

Strangely enough, it was curiosity, we are told, that moved Moses to approach the presence of God. That childlike curiosity will get us every time. That curiosity fuels our imagination, our imagination fuels our dreams, our dreams fuel our souls, and our souls inform our lives. Whether we realize it or not, everything we do is an expression of either how alive our souls are or how much we have allowed ourselves to be deadened over time.

We teach children convergent thinking and discourage divergent thinking. Convergent thinking teaches us to follow a particular set of logical steps to arrive at the one correct solution. Divergent thinking focuses on the spontaneous, free-flowing release of creativity and imagination to explore unknown paths and discover unexpected solutions. Our entire educational system is built on convergent thinking. Education has been reduced to the organization and dispensing of data. We teach our children that to excel in this world you have to be able to fill in the blanks. The worldview we transfer to our children is that there is always only one right answer to every problem, and that answer has already been discovered by your teacher. If you are to succeed, you must excel at memorizing the facts that your teacher already knows, so that one day you may teach them to someone else. The irony is that to my best understanding up to 95 percent of children naturally gravitate to divergent thinking while only 5 percent move naturally to convergent thinking. You only have to be a parent to know that children are naturally imaginative and creative and that a huge part of parenting is teaching children to color within the lines.

It seems that quickly, at least by the age of twelve, this 95:5 ratio flips and remains a constant throughout our adulthood. In contrast to children, nine out of ten adults naturally move to convergent thinking. Only a small fraction remain mentally agile enough for our own childlike imagination and curiosity to inspire and activate divergent thinking processes. Ironically, most often the adult who is perceived as a divergent thinker is considered a genius or a creative, when really all they've done is to refuse to grow up. Or perhaps a more accurate description would be that they refused to relinquish the God-given attributes given to them at birth and applied them to the great problems faced by humanity. Concerning this, Einstein noted, "The pursuit of truth and beauty is a sphere of activity in which we are permitted to remain children all our lives."

For years, we have resonated at Mosaic with a community of cultural influencers known as the Wedgwood Circle, which was founded by Mark Rodgers. This group sees the ultimate intention for humanity as expanding the good, the beautiful, and the true. It strikes me that my affection for these three arenas and for those who express them to their fullest capacity is related to my refusal to give up on childlike wonder.

I am amazed at how many people describe the fruition of their dreams as beginning in a childhood longing. There is a mysterious and beautiful relationship between the masterpiece our lives can become and the world we played in as children, where we lost ourselves in our imagination.

My friend Carrie Arcos was born in Albany, New York. She has been married for thirteen years to David Arcos, who is one of the most creative people I have ever had the privilege of working with. In many ways, they illustrate a contrast between recklessness and responsibility. David was always imagining and creating, while Carrie worked as an educator and invested her remaining energy in being a great wife and mother. Her hands were full, to say the very least, with three children between five and ten.

As long as I have known Carrie, she has had a dream of being a writer. Rarely have I met someone who knew more about literature. And while she dabbled in poetry and short stories, she never seemed quite willing to cross the line and risk a career as a novelist. Her first stab at a novel left her less than satisfied, from her own description. As she said, "I wrote a first novel and it was terrible." But she continued, "That was okay, because I needed to write it to know that I could go the distance."

Eventually she decided to write a story about her own personal journey and deep pain. Her second novel, *Out of Reach,* was inspired by her personal journey with her younger brother's addiction to methamphetamines. That she wrote it as a young adult novel is not surprising, as she spent many years as a high school teacher and always had a deep affection for her students. She spent much of her career as an educator searching for books with which her students could identify, books that could help them in some way with the real issues they confronted. Now this mother of three begins her forties with her book being a finalist for the National Book Award, a finalist for the California Book Award, and a winner of several Best Children's Book of the Year awards. It shouldn't surprise anyone that she has now completed another book, *There Will Come a Time.* The masterpiece that is her life is the beautiful culmination of years of faithfulness, determination, and courage. That's how masterpieces are forged.

I see this reality all around me—men and women who refuse to stop growing, dreaming, and risking. In some ways, it's like a second childhood with all the benefits of the wisdom accumulated over time. You need both the wisdom and the wonder for your life to become a masterpiece.

Corrie Sullivan was born in Ireland, is madly in love with her husband Aaron, and is the mother of two girls. Her mother was a stay-at-home mom, her father a businessman who distributed arts and crafts materials as well as serving as a pastor. Though she attended college at the National College of Art and Design in Dublin, she left university with a lack of confidence and diminished creativity. Ironically, her creative potential remained mostly dormant until she had children. "I have always been creative, and it wasn't until I had children that I realized that being creative was a necessity. After I had Sienna, I knew I couldn't just be 'a stay-at-home mother.' I needed an outlet for my creativity. It bubbled up inside of me. It came naturally to me to combine my creative endeavors with motherhood."

It was almost as if the natural wonder she saw in her daughter reawakened the wonder and creativity within her. Corrie met another stay-at-home mom in 2007. They both had a passion for kids' vintage clothing, so they started a company called Homespun Vintage. They started slowly by sourcing vintage kids' clothes from thrift stores and flea markets, and then in 2011 decided to manufacture and produce a small collection. Working around their children's schedules, they found a way to squeeze in work during nap times and evenings.

I share this not because Homespun has become a global fashion brand, because the reality is that after three years, Homespun is barely able to pay its bills. The lesson is that two friends inspired each other to begin to turn their lives into masterpieces. They have great marriages and great children; they are beautiful people who make the world better simply by living in it; and now they are venturing to express their full creative potential by adding to the beauty and wonder of the world. It shouldn't surprise us that two moms who love their kids and love making beautiful things out of discarded materials would create a children's fashion line called Homespun Vintage.

We see this all around us, from Blake Mycoskie, who decided somebody needed to put shoes on children and started TOMS, to Scott Harrison, who felt compelled to provide clean water to Africa and started one of America's top-rated organizations, Charity: Water, to my beautiful wife, Kim, who fearlessly leads teams into the depths of human suffering and tragedy in places such as Bangladesh, Tanzania, and India. All around us, there are men and women committed to living their lives passionately and courageously, never relinquishing their childlike wonder and refusing to surrender their ideals. The artisan soul believes in the best in all of us, and therefore refuses to accept anything less for themselves.

If this book is of any value at all, it is my hope that you will once again see yourself through the eyes of a child, or at the very least see that you, too, were no ordinary child—that you are, in fact, divine material. Just as the Lord God told Jeremiah that before he was born he knew him and while he was still in his mother's womb he called him out, this same truth applies to you. In the full meaning of the word, you were born a masterpiece, a work of art, an expression of the divine imagination, but you are both a work of art and an artist at work, and this is why the life you live and the choices you make are critical. We can deny who we are and say that we are not creative, we're not artistic, we're not imaginative, but this doesn't excuse us from our responsibility. You have been given a great gift, and that gift is your life. This life was never intended to just be endured or survived.

Life is a creative act. And as Henri Matisse once stated so succinctly, "creativity takes courage." The things that make us most human are the expressions of our most artistic selves. To love is humanity's greatest achievement. There is nothing in the universe more beautiful than this. While the common materials for the human experience far too often come from our experiences of pain, loss, and betrayal, it is hope that brings the bright colors to make life an indescribable work of art. And then there is the indomitable character that emerges from what would otherwise be an ordinary human being and that is forged through a life of faith. We imagine and dream, but when we are changed, we create.

This, in the end, is what makes the human species distinct from all other creatures: we are creatures of faith and hope and love. If these are the colors with which we choose to fill our pallets, if these are the hues in which we choose to dip our brushes to touch our canvases, then whatever the final product might be, whatever the world may see on the canvases of our lives, in the end the result will be the same. It will be a masterpiece, and you will know without arrogance or embarrassment that your life was your greatest work of art and that against all odds, from your first breath to your last, you never relinquished your artisan soul.

Anvil and Hammer

The artisan soul demands of us the hard work of beating out the metal into the form that expresses its greatest beauty.

We stand between the anvil and the hammer—positioning ourselves in the very place where God can form us into his work of art.

Below are practices to guide you through this creative process. Remember that you are both an artist at work and a work of art. Take time to allow God to make you a work of art, so that your life can be the most beautiful expression of your artisan soul.

Soul: The Essence of Art
The hard work of caring for our soul

- ☐ Make love the unifying principle of your life—let love inform all your motives, decisions, and actions.
- ☐ Set time apart to be alone—begin with fifteen minutes a day to decompress and reconnect with God.
- ☐ Begin a practice of prayer and reflection focused on gratitude.
- ☐ Use the Psalms as a guide to work through your emotions, questions, and aspirations.
- ☐ Allow the Scriptures to inspire you and awaken your artisan soul.
- ☐ Take time to see and absorb the beauty and wonder all around you.
- ☐ Take time to enjoy life, and make sure you laugh a lot.
- ☐ Connect to a community of faith and open up your life to others.
- ☐ Do more of the things you love and less of the things that kill your spirit.
- ☐ Spend more time with people who inspire you and less time with those who crush your spirit.
- ☐ Invest in yourself by bringing into your life voices who inspire you and refresh your spirit.

Let me invite you to join our organization's podcast at Mosaic.org/Podcast and to follow me on Twitter at @erwinmcmanus.

Voice: The Narrative That Guides
The hard work of finding our own voice

- ❐ Think through all the voices that have informed you throughout your life.
- ❐ Write down each and every person who has influenced you for good or bad.
- ❐ Identify what their narrative for your life was and how it has shaped you.
- ❐ Make an honest assessment of which of those voices have had a dominant role in shaping your internal narrative of yourself.
- ❐ Ask a few close friends to hear how you understand your story, and ask them to reflect back to you if your assessment resonates with them.
- ❐ Take time to study what the Scriptures say about who you are, and think about what your life would look like if you embraced this narrative as your own.
- ❐ Focus on what it means to be created in God's image.
- ❐ Reflect on God's declaration that you are wonderfully and marvelously made.

❐ Place into your narrative that God knew you before you were born and calls you out with intention and purpose.

❐ Decide who you want to become: What is the story you want to tell through your life?

❐ Write a declaration of who you are!

❐ Share it with at least one friend who will celebrate your new life narrative.

Interpretation: Translation of Life
The hard work of changing our perspective

❐ Begin a process to investigate how you see the world.

❐ Make two lists:
     everything good in your life;
     everything bad in your life.

❐ Now examine your lists.
     Which list is longer?
     Which list came more naturally?

❐ Is it easier for you to be pessimistic or to be optimistic?

❐ Place yourself on a scale of optimism versus pessimism.

❐ Write your life story in one page as a pessimist.

❐ Now write it in one page as an optimist.

❐ Now write it as if you were convinced that God

is at work in your life and intends only good for you.

❐ Now begin reinterpreting life through this filter: "I know the plans I have for you. Plans to prosper you and not to harm you, plans to give you hope and a future," says the Lord.

❐ Write down every good and beautiful thing that has ever happened to you.

❐ Take time to record everything you have learned and gained from your failures and hardships.

❐ Begin a practice of identifying every good and beautiful act or experience that comes your way.

❐ Train yourself to see life as a miracle by thanking God continuously for your life.

❐ See the world through God's eyes by always finding the hope and joy in every circumstance.

Image: Manifestation of Imagination
The hard work of materializing our dreams

❐ Write a manifesto declaring the kind of world you will create.

❐ Make a list of things in your imagination that would make the world better if they became a reality.

❑ Identify everything you could do now to make your life a closer reflection of the one you long to live.

❑ Make every small change you can to move your life into an expression of your passions and longings.

❑ Grab some close friends and ask them which of your ideas they think you have the most potential to make happen.

❑ Look to see if there are others who share your passion.

❑ Find a place to serve—find someone or some organization you can serve that moves you closer to living out that passion.

❑ Start small and dream big:

If you want to be a writer, write articles and share them with your friends.

If you want to be a designer, make something for your kids or as Christmas gifts for friends.

If you want to do humanitarian work, go on a short-term project to serve the underserved, either overseas or in your community.

If you want a new career, begin to volunteer during your spare time to learn a new trade.

If you want to change the world, start by making small changes to your world.

❑ Every day, identify one thing that happened in the world as a result of the choices you made!

Craft: The Elegance of Workmanship
The hard work of greatness

☐ Identify something in your life that is an extension of who you are and the work you do.

☐ Make a commitment to either stop doing it or do it to the best of your ability.

☐ Remember, if it's worth doing, it's worth doing well.

> What are you doing that is not worth doing?
> What are you doing that is worth doing but that you are not doing well?

☐ Make a list of everything you are doing that you need to stop doing.

☐ Create an exit plan and execute it.

☐ Make a list of everything you are doing that is worth your life.

☐ Evaluate the quality of your work.

☐ Ask others to give you honest feedback, telling them your standard is excellence.

☐ Remember: you may never be the best in the world, but you can give the best of yourself.

☐ Reorganize your priorities to give more time to what you do well and drop those things you do poorly.

☐ Refine your skills by working with people more skilled than yourself.

❐ Practice, practice, practice.

❐ Never stop learning—never stop growing—never stop improving!

Canvas: The Context of Art

The hard work of being human and reclaiming our humanity

❐ Check canvas:

How are your relationships?

How does your inner world look?

How does your outer world look?

❐ Check dimensions:

Are you known by love?

Are you a voice of hope?

Are you living by faith?

❐ Check material:

Take a positive attitude toward life.

Have sincere motives toward others.

Have the courage to risk and fail.

Embrace the future as an adventure.

Celebrate mystery.

Remember that people matter most.

Make life an act of worship.

❐ Embrace limits:

Eliminate everything that makes you less than the best reflection of your humanity.

Entrust yourself to God, to work with
limited material to create a timeless work of
art out of your life.

Keep your integrity bounded and your
imagination boundless.

Live a principled life so that you may be
most free to create a beautiful life.

Masterpiece: A New Humanity
The hard work of a life well lived

- ❏ May the world I touch be more beautiful and better off for my being here.
- ❏ May my life be a work of art, and may I always live as an artist at work.
- ❏ May my life be a mosaic: a work of art made up of fragmented and broken pieces brought together by the Master Artisan, who creates in me a masterpiece most perfectly reflected when his light strikes through me.
- ❏ May the world become as God alone can imagine and create.

Acknowledgments

So many people are involved whenever anything of value is created. I have the privilege of working with the best people in the world.

I want to thank the amazing team and tribe which is Mosaic. You have been such a huge part of not only this project but have lived out this creative manifesto. You are the creators of the future! You are the beginning of a new humanity where every person knows their intrinsic value and lives out their divine potential.

Thank you HarperOne. I want to especially express

my gratitude to Roger Freet, who invited me to return to this beautiful world of words, books, and ideas.

Thank you Jan Miller, Shannon Marven, and Nicki Miser at Dupree Miller for their belief in me and my voice.

I want to especially thank Holly Quillen, Alisah Duran, and Meg Miller who run command central in Los Angeles!

Thank you, to all who allowed me to share their stories. You are my inspiration!

A special thanks to Hank Fortener who not only shot the back cover photo but also leads our team at Mosaic.

I must also acknowledge the creative direction of Aaron McManus who brought the cover-photo shoot—and so much more—to life.

Thank you Kim and Mariah for being there for me when I needed you most.

Most of all I want to thank the One who saw in me what no one else could see, and what I could never hope or believe would ever be true about me.

Thank you Jesus of Nazareth for seeing me and calling me out to follow You. I will never be the same.